PROBLEMS OF POLITICAL PHILOSOPHY

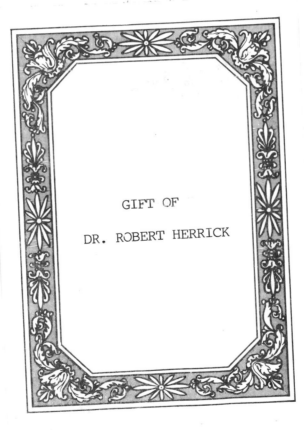

CHANDLER PUBLICATIONS IN PHILOSOPHY
Ian Philip McGreal, Editor

Problems
of
Political
Philosophy

Jean H. Faurot

Sacramento State College

89-1478

CHANDLER PUBLISHING COMPANY

An Intext Publisher · Scranton, Pennsylvania 18515

From *The Republic of Plato*, F. M. Cornford, tr. (1945), p. 318. Reprinted by permission of Oxford University Press.

From Werner Jaeger, *Paideia: the Ideals of Greek Culture*, Gilbert Highet, tr. (1945), Vol. I, p. 325. Reprinted by permission of Oxford University Press.

From Jean-Jacques Rousseau, *The Social Contract and Other Discourses*, G. D. H. Cole, tr. (Everyman's Library, No. 660), pp. 5, 13, 14, 15, 18, 19, 22, and 27. Reprinted by permission of E. P. Dutton & Co., Inc., and J. M. Dent & Sons, Ltd.

From G. W. F. Hegel, *Philosophy of Right*, T. M. Knox, tr. (1942), para. 20, 41, 44, 45, 183, 187, 207, and 246. Reprinted by permission of Oxford University Press.

From John Dewey, *Individualism Old and New* (1930), pp. 82, 99, and 119; *Liberalism and Social Action* (1935), pp. 56 ff.; *Freedom and Culture* (1939), p. 141. Reprinted by permission of Putnam's.

From John Dewey, *The Public and Its Problems* (1927), pp. 27, 33, 54, 55, 57, 67, 149, 150, and 166. Reprinted by permission of the Swallow Press, Chicago: copyright 1954.

TO MY FATHER

CONTENTS

CONTENTS

FOREWORD

The aim of this book, like that of other volumes in this series, is to introduce the beginning student to the philosophical way of thinking by confronting him with the fundamental problems of Western philosophy and by showing him the different ways in which representative thinkers have tried to resolve them. The problems of political philosophy considered here are summarily designated under the headings of *order, freedom, justice,* and *history*. After an introductory chapter which explores the problems in contemporary terms, a chapter is devoted to each of nine major political thinkers from Plato to Dewey. Each chapter is divided into four sections, with one section devoted to each of the four problems dealt with in the Introduction. Although each chapter is very nearly a self-contained essay and can be read by itself, the reader is advised to begin with Chapter I; furthermore, especially if he is new to philosophy, he is advised not to skip the chapters on Plato and Aristotle.

To Professor Ian P. McGreal, editor of this series, goes the credit for originating the plan which I have followed. This acknowledgment, however, is but a small part of the debt which I owe him for his inspiration and criticism through the many years we have worked as colleagues. Of the others whom I well might credit, I mention only Professor Robert G. Thompson of the Department of Government, Sacramento State College, and my wife, Louise, the ideal reader.

J. H. F.

Sacramento State College

ix

PROBLEMS OF POLITICAL PHILOSOPHY

I

❦

FOUR PROBLEMS
for the
PHILOSOPHER

William James once rather informally characterized philosophy as an unusually strenuous effort to think things through. In a more formal vein he explained that he meant to emphasize "thinking about things in the most comprehensive possible way," or "thinking about generalities rather than about particulars."[1]

But most of our thinking starts with particulars and ends with particulars. This method is especially prominent in politics. Most politicians are interested in winning particular elections and in seeing particular laws enacted. Adapting the language of warfare, we talk of political *campaigns*, and we call the men who plan the campaigns *strategists*. A good strategist has to think things through; his thinking runs from particulars to particulars. He has to consider what the consequences of this or that particular course of action will be in view of different eventualities. Although he must often use generalities, they are not his main concern.

But most political groups have not only strategists but also *theorists*, persons who are mainly concerned with issues. Theorists study

1

the literature of politics and engage in general discussions. They are less interested in the results of polls and in the selection of the right candidate than they are in writing certain principles into the platform. A good theoretician has to think things through, but he deals less with particulars than with generalities. According to James's definition, the theorist is on his way to becoming a philosopher. The political theorist may even use the terms *philosophy* and *theory* nearly interchangeably, and he may speak of his philosophy of government or his philosophy of the state. But whether or not he becomes a philosopher in any important sense depends upon how he deals with generalities. Does he customarily reason from generalities (concerning, for example, the right to freedom of speech, or the right to self-defense) to particular applications of the rule? If so, no matter how strenuously he thinks, he is not philosophizing. Only the person who develops his generalities into still more comprehensive ideas, who is puzzled by ambiguities (for example, in talking about freedom), and who wants, as far as possible, to see politics in broadly human, or even cosmic, terms, can be said to have genuinely philosophical concerns. It is fairly certain, in fact, that one who has these characteristics will not confine himself to philosophizing about politics but will raise the same kind of questions about science, religion, art, language, education, or whatever other matter of human interest comes to his attention.

A philosopher cannot afford to lose all touch with particulars. If his subject is politics, he must deal with matters of genuine political concern; and if what he says is to have any interest to others, he must speak out of the experience of his own time and place. In other words, the problems of political philosophy originate as problems of practical politics.

Among the pressing problems of our day, two — the problem of freedom and the problem of justice — have never been far from the center of man's concern. A recent writer[2] argues that the planned society of the future will have justice for all but freedom for none. Whether this statement is true or false, it reminds us that freedom and justice are still living issues. At the same time it alerts us to broader considerations that usually go unnoticed. The great political fact of our time is change, change so tremendous as to render questionable the very existence of political life in the future. For this reason, I have placed two further problems alongside the problems of freedom and justice. One is the problem of order — not merely the practical problem of preserving order, but the theoretical one of determining the range of possibilities of political order. The other is the problem of history — what change means to man and how far it is subject to his control.

It must be kept in mind that the philosopher's interest in political problems is not the same as the citizen's or the statesman's. For example, the history of modern democracy has been in large part a struggle to secure greater freedom for more people. The practical problem for our founding fathers was to devise a system of government with built-in safeguards against tyranny. Since that time political problems have turned on various issues, such as slavery, woman's suffrage, and civil rights.

The practical problem of freedom, how to get freedom and how to keep it, is based on the assumption that everyone knows what freedom is and considers it desirable. But philosophers have long been troubled as to what it is that men cherish under the name of freedom. Is the proverbial unspoiled savage free, and does man lose his freedom when he is prevented from keeping pigs in his yard and is compelled to pay taxes? Here is a problem that calls not for action but for thought. Moreover, it is not the kind of problem that can be resolved by factual investigation because this problem has to do with a state of mind, not with a state of affairs. The philosopher's problem is to unravel the confusions that result when men talk about such matters as freedom and justice without having thought through what they are.

ORDER

Order is one of those matters of which we have no awareness until something goes wrong. Tornados and earthquakes make us aware of natural order, muscle cramps and sprains make us aware of physical order; power failure, unemployment, and air raids make us aware of social order.

Political order is an aspect of social order, but it is one aspect only. It is the aspect we are likely to think of first in a crisis because the moment disorder appears we find ourselves saying "There ought to be a law!" and "Where are the police?" At the same time, we know that passing laws and increasing the police force are no solutions if the people have no willingness to obey. Political order presupposes economic and social order.

The political order — or as we customarily say, the state — consists of individuals who, besides being members of the state, are also members of numerous other associations, some hereditary and some voluntary. Many of these associations bear more directly upon men's lives and fortunes than does the state, with its foundation of law and sovereignty. Nevertheless, states have peculiar functions that other associations cannot perform, and the welfare of the larger community demands that these distinctive functions be correctly understood. The first problem of political philosophy, therefore, is to define the state. *What is the political bond? What distinguishes the state from other forms of human association? What constitutes the political order?*

One way to answer these questions might be to review our experience of what is undoubtedly one of the most impressive political systems ever devised. This method, however, would be like trying to understand the principles of the automobile by looking under the hood of a modern motor car — a simpler machine would serve our purpose better. Thus, to get at the heart of politics, let us forget our own nation and consider the problems facing a new or emerging nation — a situation real enough in many parts of the world today — and let us ask ourselves what a political adviser would have to do to get such a nation running. It is easy to imagine what steps the military man would want to take, or the educator, or the industrial engineer. Our special question, however, is what steps the political expert would want to take.

Presumably a political adviser would support the soldier's determination to restrain troublemakers, the educator's projects for building up the peoples' characters and informing their minds, and the engineer's attempts to put them to work. But as one who is persuaded of the importance of the political structure of a nation, our expert would not be satisfied until he had pulled the people together, given them a sense of community, and enabled them to take over the direction of their affairs. We will have to suppose that he would be sufficiently broad-minded to recognize that not all peoples require the same form of government, and that he would be sensitive enough to cultural values to let the nation follow its own basic aspirations. At the same time, the political expert would have to make the people understand the essential features of the political order — that in some sense it rests upon acceptance of an ideal, that it cannot be imposed by force, and that it is not a result of education or of scientific planning.

In order for politics to function, men must acquire a sense of community, a faith in what they can achieve by working together, and a willingness to submerge their personal ambitions in the larger enterprise. Of course, no state has ever crystallized around ideals as abstract as these terms suggest. Men usually unite around the ancestral claims of some clan or leader, in support of territorial claims, or in opposition to foreign domination. If they are to form a political union, they must be of one mind on certain issues, but on other matters they may hold back, reserving ancient prerogatives or newly won liberties for other groups. Ordinarily they will have decided opinions as to who is and who is not suited to be the head of state. They may also insist on having a voice in making important decisions. All of these considerations enter into the understanding which constitutes a political bond, and which, indeed, is commonly called a constitution.

It is probable that the imaginary approach to the problem of order will meet with objections. Someone may say that in making politics rest on the consent of the governed, we have introduced a dogma peculiar to democracy and have lost touch with political reality, which always rests on power, even in democracies. This objection has validity. But to understand politics, one must be aware of the different kinds of power. Our question is *What distinguishes a ruler from a tyrant?* Or, more generally, *What is the special character of political power?* The answer lies in the notion of legitimacy or right. The ruler has the right to use force provided that he does so at the behest of and on behalf of the people. A kind of order is presupposed here — an ideal order which exists in men's minds. Where political order is well established, little doubt exists as to the right and wrong exercise of power; and where order has been disturbed, the notion of legitimacy is obscured. Nonetheless, the emergence of a new political power requires some formulation of the idea of right, which must then slowly find acceptance in the minds of the governed.

There is something very artificial about politics, as our account makes clear. The ancient Sophists realized this fact when they insisted that the state is conventional and not natural. The state, they said, like religion, is something that exists only in men's minds, not like the family, which is rooted in physical necessity. Because the Sophists assumed that what exists in the mind has but little importance, they tended to belittle the state. Nevertheless, the observation that the state is based on convention was a profound one and underlies the distinction recognized in our times between natural commu-

nities, which are held together by customs, beliefs, and attitudes
handed down through generations, and voluntary societies, which
are formed for the realization of particular goals and organized with
these ends in view.

The peculiarity of the state, however, is that it is neither clearly a
natural community nor a voluntary association, but lies somewhere
between these two. Like a natural community, the state has traditional elements, particularly where notions of right are involved;
membership is never quite voluntary in the way that membership in
a club or business partnership is. On the other hand, states are deliberate enterprises, designed more or less consciously with specific
ends in view, limited by laws, and require special officers to carry
out their work, much in the way commercial enterprises and engi-
neering projects do. In our fast-moving times, when the wisdom of
the past seems less and less pertinent, states seem to be moving more
and more in the direction of huge corporations.

Here, then, lies the crux of the philosophical problem concerning
the political order. Tribal societies are held together by habitual
loyalties; business organizations are held together by conditional
consent. The state has some characteristics of each. Where does its
essential nature lie? As we shall see, sometimes classical political
thinkers have leaned in one direction and sometimes in the other.

FREEDOM

In the broadest sense, the problem of political freedom concerns
the relation of the state to its constituents, whether as individuals or
as other associations. But the word *freedom* has so many meanings
that it is difficult to stick to one. Let us recall the prediction –
hopefully a false one – that the planned society of the future will
allow freedom to no one, though it will secure justice for all. What
this forecast means is that in this future society the ordinary individual will have no opportunity to make decisions in matters of any
consequence; in one sense of the term, he will have no "freedom."
But part of the idea of a planned society is that people in the society
will like it that way because things will be so well arranged that
everyone will be doing what he wants to do, and all sense of constraint or compulsion will be gone. If, however, freedom sometimes
means doing what one pleases, as it surely does, then in this second
sense of the word, denizens of that planned society will have freedom as well as justice.

This ambiguity in the concept of freedom is the basis for much of the propaganda battle between the so-called freedom-loving nations and the totalitarian nations of the world. But the moral and psychological freedoms here mentioned are not really what is meant by political freedom, important as they are to political discussions. Indeed, freedom of choice and the kind of responsibility it entails are essential to the existence of the political order, as opposed to other kinds of social control, whether primitive or utopian, where the individual is not required to give his consent.

Turning to the age-long struggle for political freedom, we must first take account of the desire of tribes, cities, and nations to be independent, to be free to manage their own affairs, and not be required to pay tribute to other nations. This is a basic form of freedom, resting almost entirely upon force and circumstance. What we have called political power or authority presupposes an order of law with effective means of enforcement. But in the absence of political power, nations rely for their freedom on other kinds of power. Accordingly, freedom or independence has varying degrees, with weaker states asking for the protection of stronger states and accepting limited autonomy. This situation, which has prevailed among nations from earliest times to our own, has sometimes been called *anarchy*; that is, the absence of authority. The freedom that is here sought is the freedom that is everywhere the privilege of strength, prominence, self-sufficiency. Incidentally, we recognize and cherish this privilege on the personal level also because without some measure of strength, competence, and force of character, other kinds of freedom are empty.

Anarchic freedom, even when claimed in the name of independence or sovereignty by a city or nation, is not political freedom in the strict sense because the freedom of anarchy is based in nature and not on convention. To bring natural or anarchic freedom under some kind of control is the main purpose of politics, as it is of other kinds of social order. Political freedom brings the strength of the group to the support of the individual who, by virtue of prior understandings, qualifies for that support. Take the instance of the slave who obtains his freedom. A runaway slave may be said to have natural freedom, but he lacks political freedom. He differs from a freedman in that he has no guarantee that he will not be returned to bondage. To be a free man, in the political sense, is to enjoy a legal standing. In societies where slavery is recognized, the master has legal rights over the slave; when the slave is freed, legal rights are granted to him. This is the first meaning of political freedom.

In many societies, however, it is possible to enjoy the minimal guarantees of the free man without enjoying the full privileges of citizenship. In early Rome, the *plebeians* were not part of the *populus* and had no voice in public affairs. Generally, ancient cities were like exclusive clubs, whose members enjoyed, besides security and affluence, the satisfaction of participating together in affairs of the state. To be an Athenian or a Roman citizen in the great days of those cities was the best thing imaginable, either by those who enjoyed the privilege or by the great numbers who, though dwelling in the city, were not members of it. Thus it is hardly surprising that the word *free* received the special connotation of one who was a citizen.

The rise of modern states added another chapter to the history of freedom. The monarchies of Spain, France, and England, although tenuously rooted in the past, were new political orders. The modern state was not a comprehensive society like the ancient city. Feudal domains, walled towns, monasteries, military orders, universities, guilds, and numerous other societies provided a social fabric in which every man enjoyed carefully defined rights. Tensions within this traditional order made possible the rise of the strong, central authority that we call the state and helped to justify it. In England, for example, memories of a long civil war disposed men to support the absolutist claims of Henry VIII. But although they looked to the state to put down factions and to protect the national interest against other kingdoms, men scarcely looked to it for freedom. On the contrary, freedom came to stand for the rights that men already possessed and that the state constantly threatened. In this context, the struggle for political freedom was an effort to impose limits on the power of the state, and led to constitutional guarantees of rights that individuals and groups were unwilling to yield.

A further chapter in the struggle for political freedom is still being written in our own revolutionary times. The traditional liberties given legal recognition by modern constitutions were frequently very selective. Moreover, they were never designed to meet the needs of modern, industrial societies. Under these circumstances, laws designed to protect the freedom of some persons had the effect of limiting or taking away the freedom of others. Not surprisingly, people who have lost whatever freedoms they or their fathers once enjoyed turn to the state as their best hope of getting freedom. In their eyes, freedom has less to fear from an increase in the power of the state than it has from the unregulated power of privileged (in the legal sense) individuals and groups. Once again, therefore, political freedom comes to mean what it did in ancient cities, a benefit which the state confers. The struggle for freedom ceases to be mainly a struggle against the state and becomes a struggle for membership in the state and a chance to have a voice in its affairs.

These are some of the complexities that the philosopher has to consider in discussing freedom. Because of man's concern with personal autonomy, he has to take account of personal freedom. Because of man's social condition, he also has to take account of the problems that arise between the individual and the group. At this level, it is possible to distinguish between two kinds of freedom: autonomy that the individual guards against other individuals and against the group, sometimes called *negative freedom*; and the extension of one's powers and the security of one's estate that cooperative effort makes possible, sometimes called *positive freedom*.

To bring some system into this diversity of concerns, philosophers have raised two questions. First, they have asked what may be called a metaphysical question: How real is the vaunted autonomy of the individual? Some philosophers deny that the individual has any reality except that which he enjoys as a member of the group. Others hold that only the individual is fully real, and that society derives whatever reality it has from the will and purpose of its members. Philosophers who place the group above the individual are logically driven to view freedom in the positive sense, if they are concerned with it at all; whereas, those who place the individual above the group would seem to be driven to regard freedom negatively. But the latter have a further choice, in view of the second question: What is the value of individual autonomy? This is partly an ethical question; but whereas the ethical philosopher is concerned mainly with the value of freedom in competition with other human values, the political philosopher is more concerned with the value of one man's freedom in competition with other men's freedom and with the whole new set of values (security, affluence, opportunity, justice) to which this competition gives rise. In view of this question of values, philosophers who hold that only individuals are real are sometimes willing to place social benefits above the negative freedom to be left alone.

JUSTICE

An individual is free when he is unconstrained; but for one man to be free, others either must constrain themselves or be constrained. The political order presupposes that, in one degree or another, men have to be constrained; at the same time, it distinguishes between a constraint that is authorized and one that is not. As we have seen, the state's very existence depends upon this distinction. Principles of justice are something like the rules of a game: at times they get in a player's way; at other times they help him along. The real significance of rules does not lie in the incidental advantage that they offer one player or the other, however, but in the fact that without them there would be no game. So it is also with the moral and legal foundations of a state, which, in effect, determine when constraint is permitted and when it is not.

No issue leads more naturally from politics to philosophy than that of justice or right. The little word *Why?*, which we use when we ask for a justification, has only to be asked often enough and the disputant finds himself on philosophical grounds. The public official who is called upon to explain his actions can usually justify himself by citing a statute or a precedent or a recognized principle, such as national security. Those who remain dissatisfied with his actions may merely question whether the actions in question are justified on these grounds or they may raise further questions as to why the particular statute or principle deserves to be followed. Finally men will find themselves arguing such questions as *Why do we have laws?* and *What is the reason for having states?* It is not difficult to see that merely asking these questions borders on impiety. Ancient peoples commonly believed that states were founded by the gods. For men to ask questions about them seemed both absurd and wicked. But when institutions break down and religious beliefs grow dim, men look to something for guidance. More or less deliberately they set up reason as their teacher and equate the reasonable with the right.

The connection between reason and justice is a remarkable one, one that is not always noticed. Man's reason characteristically seeks out necessary connections. One way he does this is to use principles or laws that apply to two or more things by virtue of the characteristics that they have in common. This is the reasoning ordinarily employed in modern science — drawing inferences from particulars to universals, and vice versa. Another way of reasoning is by attending to the steps that are necessary to reach a desired end. This is the reasoning ordinarily employed in arts and crafts — reasoning from ends to means.

There is nothing sophisticated about either of these kinds of reasoning: children frequently excel in both. A younger child demands to know why he does not get a bicycle when his older brother does. If he can be led to see the respect in which he and his brother differ — that they fall in different classes with respect to bicycles — he may be contented; however, it will probably be difficult to show him that he is not entitled to have something to ride because he knows that he is human, and he readily observes that all human beings have something to ride. In this matter the child uses the logic of universals and particulars. He is also capable of using the logic of ends and means. If he is asked to forgo a certain satisfaction, he wants to know why; but he may yield the point if he can be shown that he must do this so that his mother can get well. That explanation makes it all right. Fortunately for parents, children are easily distracted. If one of them comes back to these concerns when he grows up, he becomes a philosopher.

Some philosophers are more bold than others in their pursuit of rational explanation. As we have seen, political order rests on convention; but is order a purely human invention, or does it grow out of some natural necessity? Those philosophers who are persuaded on general grounds that the world as a whole follows intelligible necessity will commonly try to fit the state into the total picture and thereby make the reasons that explain the one also serve for the other. For example, those who view nature organically, as a whole made up of mutually interdependent parts, will apply the same principles to the state; those who view nature as the product of mechanical forces operating independently of any design or pattern follow a similar procedure.

Philosophers who concern themselves with the ultimate nature and order of things are called *metaphysicians*, and the theories with which they attempt to justify the state by situating it in the world order are called *metaphysics*. We have called these philosophers bold, and so they are in what they hope to accomplish. On the other hand, measured by the distance that separates their thinking from prephilosophical understanding of the state, they seem timid because the urge to found the state on cosmic principles was what led ancient men to propound political myths.

Those philosophers who have less confidence in man's ability to find ultimate truths, as well as those who hold that a sharp discontinuity exists between nature and man, reject metaphysical theories of the state and content themselves with theories that we may call *ethical*. For example, those who regard human behavior as essentially goal-directed will justify the state as a more or less intelligent means of attaining normal human ends; but those who think of man as a uniquely personal being, guided by a conscience and concerned with inner rectitude, will justify the state as a means of safeguarding moral principles. Such theories stay closer to our ordinary thinking about justice than do those that try to square politics with metaphysics. Thus when we ask whether certain government measures are justified or not, we want to know whether they are necessary in view of acknowledged goals; although we sometimes say that decisions or laws are unjust without asking about their consequences, merely on the ground that they offend our sense of fairness or that they are inhumane. Those who develop ethical theories of the state are merely giving these ways of thinking their most general statement.

In view of its connection with reason, justice emphasizes the universal, in contrast to freedom, which emphasizes the particular; or in the other perspective, justice is concerned primarily with the good of the whole, as distinct from the particular values of its individual members. Some kind of justice is essential to any association to which free men give assent, from the simplest and most impoverished tribal society to the richest and most complicated industrial nation. That justice is the special preoccupation of states is mainly due to the intermediate condition in which states stand, between the natural order of the family and the purely artificial order say, of a business organization. We mentioned that, although states embody many of the features of the voluntary association in that they envisage definite ends and set up suitable machinery to accomplish those ends, nevertheless they carry over many features of traditional societies, particularly the feelings of loyalty and respect that mainly constitute the political bond.

It is instructive, in this connection, to compare states with business organizations, and political justice with business ethics. Now, as anyone who has ever played Monopoly knows, business is essentially amoral. Where organizations are concerned, the maxim holds that the end justifies the means. If it is considered out of its social context and made a law to itself, any business, or any organization is immoral; and the reason most organizations do observe certain decencies is that they have for their members men and women who are already committed to moral ideals, together with the fact that organizations usually have need to cultivate the good will of the larger community where moral standards are respected. It is this situation which gives rise to the problems of business ethics.

States have similar problems. Because they superimpose special ends and special organizations on a social order already constituted by custom, states are always faced with ethical problems. Sophocles' tragedy *Antigone* dramatizes this conflict. Antigone insists, in the name of custom sanctified by religion, which she calls a higher law, that she must bury the body of her brother Polynices, even though he has been a traitor to the state. King Creon, taking his stand on the requirements of statecraft, demands that the guilty man receive the extreme penalty. Creon is right in his general contention — whatever fault there may be in its particular application — that in order to enjoy the benefits of a state, its members must surrender some of their private scruples. But Antigone is also right in pressing the claims of ancestral piety; and, in spite of certain flaws of character, she is a heroine to all who see in political necessity a perennial threat to justice of a more fundamental sort.

HISTORY

Past and future are always tugging at each other in the political order. Conservatives view with dismay the changes that the onward march of civilization introduces into the life of the community and demand that the state protect traditional values. Progressives eagerly embrace the benefits of new knowledge and new techniques; moreover, they want to use the power of the state to accelerate this change. All progressives believe that once man has thrown off his old prejudices and learned to think reasonably, society will enter an age of peace and prosperity unlike anything hitherto known, but they differ as to whether this change can be accomplished within the framework of existing states or whether it requires special totalitarian states designed to destroy the old and bring in the new.

That political thought has to take account of change is not surprising. In a sense, politics and history are twins. Primitive societies are called *prehistorical* (as well as *prepolitical*), not merely because the historian has no materials for reconstructing historical events, but more especially because primitive cultures, patterned closely on the rhythms of nature, were designed to prevent anything from happening that would alter the routines of society. What we understand by an historic event, one that ushers in significant change, was to early societies what illness or injury is to the human body: all the resources of the primitive group were marshalled to heal the disorder and to restore normalcy.

History proper begins for any community when, unable to assimilate changes through minute adjustments in its beliefs and habits, it must create a special governing agency. This alteration invariably happens when a folk society becomes urbanized or, as we say, civilized. The science and technology that make possible the highly organized life of cities is a constant source of change and is, perhaps, the only part of a culture with a built-in tendency to develop. Economic and social structures, moral and religious beliefs do not develop naturally; but the increase in wealth, the appearance of new occupations and new classes, the confrontation through trade and war with other cities put intolerable strain on social institutions and demand change. Such is the substance of history, even as it is the milieu in which states are founded and become established. When traditional controls are no longer adequate, a society must submit the administration of its interests and the enforcement of its demands to a particular group that knows how to bring technical reason to bear quickly and effectively upon the problems created by change. As we have seen, the political order is intermediate between a natural society and an organization, incorporating elements of each. Political order is a product of change, and many of its functions are directed toward meeting change. When, as sometimes happens, a culture arrests technical advance, it becomes static and tends to lose its political structure even as it drops out of history.

These reflections on the connection between politics and history are not in themselves metaphysical or even philosophical: they are more like the observations we expect from anthropologists and sociologists. They become philosophical only when men go on to understand them by reference to some divine plan or to see them as instances of some general tendency of nature. For example, the theory of cyclical return envisages history as a fall from innocence and sees conditions as getting worse and worse until the race has to be exterminated and a new start made. This view prevailed among ancient peoples, who never quite lost the primitive man's sense of reverence for nature and who tended to regard man's growing dominion as presumptuous. The opposite theory, the theory of progress, champions civilization and affirms man's dominion over nature. It sees in the primitive condition only ignorance and bondage, and it looks to reason to bring man truth and mastery. At first the belief in progress rested on the vision of inspired teachers, who proclaimed that God created the world with a view to making men happy; modern humanists, however, are more likely to connect it with the theory of organic evolution and to place their hope in the further development of human intelligence.

We have tended to call such theories *philosophies*, but it is more useful, when they impinge upon politics, to call them *ideologies*. The point of considering them at all lies in the fact that, when they are taken seriously, they lay an extra burden on the state. If our account is correct, the traditional moral order and the voluntary, technical order are both present in the political order. Pragmatic thinkers are content that it should remain this way, but ideologists think otherwise. Looking either to the prehistoric past or to the posthistoric future, they want the state to work for its own dissolution; that is to say, they want to eliminate either the technical or the moral order.

The problem of history, for the political philosopher, is the problem of political religion, or the problem of ideology. What is the purpose of politics? Do states have a transcendent reference? Is there a pattern in history which, because it overrides ordinary political wisdom, ought to be the chief concern of political man? Ought the state to put itself under the tutelage of some church, some party, or some academic discipline which possesses arcane knowledge of the future? Or are these claims to transcendence illusory and are all the misery and destruction that they entail merely an added burden to the normal toll of suffering that history exacts? The contemporary philosopher often finds ideologies disagreeable to contemplate and passes them by in silence, but he does so at the risk of falsifying the picture of political thought. No state has ever been without its myths, not to speak of its delusions of grandeur; nor are these elements absent from political philosophy. Our account of the state has hitherto been factual and pragmatic. We have assumed that man is a reasonable creature and that he enters into the political order intelligently, understanding something of its dangers as well as its utility. Politics, however, has never been quite that rational. Early man sought meaning in divine archetypes, which he preferred to emulate rather than to attend to his practical needs. When the old archetypes were no longer helpful, it was inevitable that his offspring should invent new ones and find it more meaningful to serve them than to apply their energies to matters at hand. Man needs something to live for, some idea to sustain him through suffering and defeat, something that does not die, as men do, and that has a chance of enduring even when states fail.

   This chapter has discussed the problems of political philosophy without reference to particular philosophers; instead, it has tried to single out the most important theoretical issues and to make them intelligible in the light of experience today. As we approach the teachings of the classic thinkers, it may be useful to restate the four problems as questions. Having in view the problem of order, we ask each philosopher to consider *Is the state natural or artificial?* To get his view on freedom, we ask *Is the state prior to the individual?* Concerning justice, *Why should I obey the state?* And, as to history, *Can man do without the state?* Because the issues we have raised are many sided, these questions must be used with circumspection. They are used here merely to open the way to a fuller understanding of the problems.

II

PLATO

Philosophy began as an attempt to find a more reasonable explanation for the origin of the world than had previously been given in myths. A fanciful, dreamlike account of beginnings was replaced by one that better agreed with the waking experience of a people well advanced in various practical arts and in such sciences as astronomy and geometry.

Early philosophers rejected the notion of a divine craftsman because it retained too much of the mythical feeling; still, their own thinking was dominated by the human craftsman's distinction between matter and form. Their aim was, first, to discover a single primary element present in all things; and, second, to find a kind of causality by means of which the multiplicity of things could be understood.

Modern writers sometimes say that such philosophical speculation was the beginning of science, but we must not forget that these early theories had no experimental basis. Logic, on the other hand, matured rapidly. It soon appeared that, because he desired intelligibility, the philosopher had better attend to form than to matter. One theory after another was discarded because it involved contradictions, until little remained to philosophy except dialectic, a method first made famous by Zeno the Eleatic and later perfected by the Sophists and by the Socratic school, who applied it not merely to the physical world but also to art, education, and politics.

Philosophy did not begin at Athens, as we might suppose, although like many other things in the classic age, it came at last to this focus of enlightenment and progress. Athens' eminence was primarily political: her experiments in what we would call participational democracy made her alert and responsive and brought to her wealth and power. During her great years, a succession of dramatic poets were her best teachers of politics and morals, although she was never especially friendly to philosophers. Hence it is ironic that we remember her for Socrates, whom she condemned to death, and for Plato, who became almost an exile after that event.

Unlike his teacher Socrates, who was of humble birth, Plato belonged to an aristocratic family. In less troubled times he would certainly have taken an active part in Athenian politics, but the death of Socrates ended that possibility. Plato went abroad, studied mathematics and philosophy with different masters, and lived for a while at the court of the tyrant Dionysius at Syracuse. When he returned to Athens, it was to establish his own school, the celebrated Academy, which drew students from all over the Greek world. Besides teaching, Plato wrote for the literate public a series of philosophical playettes, or dialogues, converting dialectic into a quasi-dramatic form and applying it to about the same range of subjects as that now covered by educational television.

The *Republic* is a book-length dialogue devoted to proving that the just man is happier than the unjust man. In order to make plain the nature of justice and of happiness, Socrates, who is the narrator as well as the chief speaker, discusses the ideal city.

ORDER

When we posed the question whether the state is natural or artificial, we asked it against the background of our earlier observation that states have some features of early tribal societies and some features of business organizations. We mentioned that some philosophers are more impressed with the customary and others with the organizational aspects of the state. What would Plato say?

An easy way to answer this question is to point to the parts of Plato's *Republic* that give his blueprint for the ideal city. The residents of this city are divided into three classes: the producers (farmers, mechanics, tradesmen), the auxiliaries (soldiers, civil servants),

and the guardians (government). Children receive elementary education in common: the less promising ones become producers and the
more promising ones, who receive special training, are initiated into
the class of auxiliaries. Of the latter group, the most promising continue their studies and become members of the governing elite. To
render them more effective, the auxiliary and guardian classes form a
caste apart: members of these classes do not marry but are bred like
animals to produce the best offspring, they have no property, and
they live together in military-type barracks. Surely, no planner ever
made a more strenuous effort to wipe the slate clean, as far as
tradition is concerned, and make a fresh beginning. Now the answer
to our question seems obvious. Plato believes that the state is an
artificial body, or at least he believes that a planned state run by
masters of the science and art of politics is the ideal to which existing states should try to conform.

Easy answers, however, are suspect when it comes to interpreting
the dialogues of Plato. For one thing, his chief spokesman, Socrates,
is notorious for his use of irony; for another, the whole aim of the
dialectic that Socrates practices is to pull the rug out from under
anyone who loves simple answers. The closer we examine his pattern
of the state, the more we begin to wonder whether it is a model of
anything. All we can be sure of is that it is an imaginary construction
and that it is meant to shed light on certain ethical questions, notably, whether it is possible for the unjust man to be happy. Evidently
Plato believes that he could not speak adequately about personal
morality except in a social context; thus, with many bold and entertaining flourishes, he constructs a model society. But whether the
model is meant to do more than illuminate the question of justice
and happiness is not quite certain, in spite of (or even because of!)
Socrates' insistence that it might someday come to pass.

In any case, Socrates' celebrated invention is not a state in the
same sense that the term has for modern totalitarian planners. Plato
distinguishes, as the Greeks commonly did and as we in the West also
do (when we do not forget), between the political society or state
and the society at large. The Greek word *polis*, translated either as
city or *state* is ambiguous because it could signify the country and
its people or it could signify the minority of people who were citizens in the full sense — usually the landowners, who were also the
militia, and who had a voice in government. In Socrates' model city,
the two upper classes constitute the state and the regimented life
applies to them alone. Nothing is said about regulating the lives of

the productive classes, who are an important part of society but who are not part of the state. Socrates' plan is scarcely anything more than a scheme for making the best possible citizens out of the men and women (including women was a great novelty) who exercise political responsibility in the midst of the larger polis.

What Socrates gives us is less a blueprint of an ideal society than a functional analysis of any society that happens to be sufficiently complex to include a political order. He explains that what is ordinarily called the city encompasses three different human concerns, only one of which, in the strict sense, is political. It is to make these distinctions clear that he develops his fictitious city. Originally the economic city stood alone as a community of farmers, artisans, and tradesmen, whose products sufficed for the satisfaction of their common needs. Socrates pictures this condition as a rustic paradise in which men were content without pursuing unnecessary desires or competing for honor or position. All the same, this is more like an animal society than a city of men.

When men introduced freedom into this necessitous city, new problems arose that could not be solved by economic means. It must have laws and men to enforce them, and it must be prepared to defend itself against covetous neighbors. This was the beginning of the political city or state. To make its functions clear, as opposed to those of the economic city, Socrates represents the state as a distinct class within the city, standing guard like a watchdog over the whole community. The guardians, as they are to be called, are guided by aims that differ from those which guide the farmer and the weaver. They are political men, with the security and the peace of the community as their special concern, and with their own art, the political art, which requires training and fidelity for its exercise.

In the ideal polity, guardians are instilled from childhood with a love of goodness and beauty, so that virtuous conduct is habitual to them and laws restricting them can be reduced to a minimum. They are bound together by familial ties, regard their fellows as parents and brethren, and hold all things in common. Moreover, they understand the necessity for leaders and followers, and they know how to take their turns at either commanding or obeying. Such is the political order. The needs to which it ministers are not the animal needs of the economic community; they are needs specific to man, whose impulses and desires are inadequately controlled by nature and must be brought under the guidance of reason.

Rising out of the guardian class, but without ceasing to be a part of it, is a third class of independent thinkers, who henceforth will be called guardians (par excellence) and the others henceforth will be known as auxiliaries. The political city or state, ever on the lookout for leaders, holds the doors of higher education open to them. The results, however, are something that the state could not anticipate. Encouraged to move beyond political beliefs and practical sciences and to acquaint themselves with the most general truths, these bright young men and women experience a kind of conversion, a revaluation of values. For them, the specifically political ends – the interests of the city – pale by comparison with the goods of philosophy; and those who have beheld the latter are tempted to retire from politics to enjoy their new luxury. Fortunately, however, they are capable of understanding the need for the state, and they will not neglect their duty, either to command or to obey.

In the framework of Socrates' ideal republic, the special features of the political order become apparent. Unlike the economic order, in which every man looks out for his own good or at most for the good of his immediate household, the political order is concerned with the good of the entire city. The good that it pursues is not prosperity or riches, but peace and harmony, an atmosphere of goodwill and trust. We may say that when men are organized politically, it is with a view to pursuing an ideal good: whereas when they are organized economically, it is in order to pursue a material good. But to be motivated to pursue the ideal good requires special training; and, in fact, education is the main concern in the development of a citizen class. Nothing is more important in achieving this end than that citizens be imbued with a love and respect for civic goals. Men who merely pursue their own desires, whether necessary or unnecessary, can never qualify as members of a political order. They will always be watching for some way to take advantage of other men, and they must be controlled by fear and by force. The citizen (we are speaking of the ideal citizen, for only by abstracting his essential quality can we hope to understand what it means to be a citizen and a member of a state) must love justice and peace with all the force of his character, even as the well-trained farmer loves a good stand of grain or the cabinetmaker a graceful piece of furniture. This attitude requires special education from childhood, a social environment suited to protect the potential citizen from falling into acquisitive and selfish habits, and, in due time, training in the arts of warfare and of government so that the concerns of the city as a whole will be cared for no less expertly than are the concerns of its various parts.

Socrates' auxiliary and guardian classes, in effect, comprise the political order. The bond that unites them is the political bond, the ideal of peace and justice, inculcated into men's souls from childhood so that it becomes a kind of second nature. Whether this bond should be called natural or artificial, as we proposed to inquire, is not quite clear. Civic loyalty, according to Socrates, must replace family loyalty; but the devotion of citizens to the state must be of the same kind as the loyalty that members of a family ordinarily feel toward each other. In other words, the political order is not held together by the deliberate purpose of men who have calculated its advantages and found that these outweigh its disadvantages. The state is an organization with specific ends, as the members of the philosophical elite understand most perfectly because they possess the science of politics. (Hence, according to Socrates, the ideal governor is the philosopher-king.) But the state is not held together by understanding alone, as those Sophists held who argued that it is based on a mutual contract between self-serving men. In that view, the state would clearly be artificial, like a business partnership. Socrates believes that the state is a great deal more than an artificial agreement, that only as men rise above desire and self-interest can they truly be said to be members of the state, and that this moral transformation is less the result of deliberate choice than it is of wise civic upbringing.

FREEDOM

The problem of freedom has to do with the relationship between society and its members, particularly between the state and those who owe it obedience. Our question, whether the individual or the state comes first, is meant to shed light on this connection. Plato's analysis gives us a good opportunity to come to grips with the problem because each social class will tend to view the matter differently.

A member of the economic class would put the individual before the state and private good before public interest. For the subpolitical man, the state, like the weather, is something alien, if not hostile. His ingenuity is challenged to get from it the most he can while giving to it as little as possible. He favors the use of force to restrain other people from harming him, but he opposes its use to keep him from harming others. He always holds his own good uppermost. The only freedom he cherishes is the freedom of anarchy. When he engages in any kind of political action, his interest is factional.

The citizen, who owes a great deal to the state, has a quite different view of freedom. As far as the citizen (auxiliary or guardian) is concerned, the state precedes the individual, both in the sense that its institutions have made the individual what he is, and in the sense that its interests have priority over those of the individual. When one of Socrates' interlocutors thought it strange that the guardians did not use their position to enrich themselves, Socrates pointed out that the purpose of the state is not to minister to the demands of this or of that class, but to look out for the interest of the community as a whole. To drive this point home, he recommended that the citizen classes should have no families, no private dwellings, and no personal wealth — the moral being that citizens as citizens have all things in common. In other words, there can be no state save where the interests of the whole society take precedence over the interests of individuals and of other groups.

How does this rule apply to the philosopher? Like other citizens, he is molded by that great civilizer, the state: there could never have been a Socrates or a Plato except for Athens. But having brought his soul under the discipline of a higher truth than any that the city is able to impart, the philosopher attains a kind of independence unknown to political man, much less to economic man. From the vantage point of philosophy, the individual takes precedence over the state; but the philosopher views the individual not merely as a producer and consumer, nor as a member of society, but as an immortal soul temporarily imprisoned in a body and rehabilitated by means of the regimen of the state.

To make the last point clear, Plato has Socrates draw a parallel between the three classes in the city and the three parts of every human soul: the appetites, the spirited part (the seat of courage and devotion), and the reason. In infancy, we are all members of the subpolitical class because our lives are dominated by the passionate part of our souls. As adolescents, when we develop our loyalty to the group and to its code, an allegiance so fundamental to the state, we are dominated by the spirited part. When we reach adulthood and must exercise independent judgment that affects not merely our own lives but also the lives of others, we are dominated by the rational part. In most of us, unfortunately, this maturity is tentative and insecure, and even after we have reached adulthood we slip back into the lower frames. Indeed, some people never seem to outgrow a juvenile preoccupation with the satisfaction of desires, and because the mutual obligations required by the political order never become

binding for them, they must be treated as wards of the state and
kept in line by threats of force. Plato makes it clear that for every
man the goal is to bring his appetites and emotions under the control
of reason, and that only when he has attained this goal can he claim
to be free.

> It is better for everyone, we believe, to be subject to a power of
> godlike wisdom residing within himself, or, failing that, imposed
> from without, in order that all of us, being under one guidance,
> may be so far as possible equal and united. This, moreover, is
> plainly the intention of the law in lending its support to every
> member of the community, and also of the government of child-
> ren; for we allow them to go free only when we have established
> in each one of them as it were a constitutional ruler, whom we
> have trained to take over the guardianship from the same prin-
> ciple in ourselves.[1]

Plato thus takes his place at the head of a long line of political
philosophers who think of freedom as a spiritual achievement and
who hold that the main purpose of the state is to raise men from a
kind of animal existence, mistakenly called freedom, so that they
can exercise the freedom of rational beings. On these assumptions,
the state is not ultimately prior to the individual. The economic man
will feel that the state is trying to take priority, and he will resist it
as far as he can. The political man will feel that the state really is
prior to the individual, because insofar as he takes seriously his
responsibilities as a citizen, he does subordinate his personal interests
to those of the state. The man whose reason has attained philosophical stature knows that the individual is prior to the state and that
even when the state places its goals above those of its members it
does so in order that its members may attain their highest personal
development.

In the history of political thought, this position is directly opposed to those schools of thought that look upon the adult human
being as naturally independent and free and that regard the state as a
contract entered into by consenting adults for limited purposes. The
latter group rejects the claim of Plato's philosopher to possession of
some unique spiritual good, and they refuse to put their necks into
the yoke by which he hopes to set them free. For these champions
of liberty, freedom consists in being allowed to live one's life without any restraint by one's fellow men; or, because that is not quite
possible, in being allowed to take part in deciding what restraints

one must accept. In Plato's time this so-called negative freedom already had its philosophical defenders. The difference between the two positions comes down to this question: granted that the advantages of life in the city depend on the development of special skills and organizations, is a special art and a special organization required to shape man into something fully human?

Plato's opponents say no. They hold that art and organization, its auxiliary, apply only to things and not to persons. Although an art and organization is suited, say, to defending a city, none is suited to making a man virtuous and happy.

On the other hand, those who agree with Plato and who regard freedom as a positive achievement answer affirmatively. There is, they say, a goal toward which all men are striving, and this goal can be known. The greatest need men have, therefore, is for specialists trained in the art and science of human well-being and for organizations to bring the benefits of this knowledge to the greatest possible number of people. Such is the philosophical issue connected with political freedom as it divides men down to our own times.

JUSTICE

The question *Why should I obey the state?* may mean *Why should someone tell me what to do?* or *Why should I not do what I want?* When this is what the question means, one way to deal with it is to let the questioner see whether he really knows what it is he wants to do. The original Socratic dialectic was designed to do just that. In the opening book of the *Republic*, Socrates relates a discussion between himself and Thrasymachus, a young man who argues that the way to be happy is not to let anyone hinder one from satisfying his own desires and who maintains that there is nothing wrong with injustice because justice is merely the name which strong men give to the rules that they are able to impose on the weak. Socrates' questions are designed to show that a man falls into contradictions when he thinks that he can let his desires lead him; that unless he exercises judgment and restraint, he will soon find himself tied up in knots; and that unless he learns to respect the aspirations of other men, most of the things he wants will pass forever beyond his reach.

The dialogue with Thrasymachus, however, is merely the introduction to the long discussion which follows, a discussion between

Socrates and two other young men, the brothers Glaucon and Adeimantus. The brothers are less radical than Thrasymachus, for although they have been impressed with the usual arguments for amoralism and are unable to answer them, their commitment to accepted morality remains unshaken. For them, the question *Why should I obey the state?* is a request for reasons they can give to support their commitment. Strictly speaking, the question of obeying the state is neither asked nor answered in the *Republic*; rather the question is *Why should I be moral?*

Glaucon puts the issue acutely: Is justice something desirable simply as an end, like pleasure, or simply as a means, like hard work, or is it desirable both as an end and as a means, like a meal that is both appetizing and nourishing? Socrates undertakes to show that the latter is the case: as an end, justice ranks so high that if necessary, one ought to suffer the loss of every other good rather than to commit an injustice; nevertheless, the world is so ordered that only through justice can one attain the goods that are necessary for happiness. Glaucon and Adeimantus are delighted with Socrates' uncompromising declaration on behalf of absolute morality and press him to give them reasons in support of his position. Before he does so, however, Socrates wants to know what justice is; and it is this inquiry that leads him to the analysis of the city and to his parallel analysis of the human soul.

In the introductory chapter, after showing the connection between what is just and what is reasonable, we mentioned that there are two general ways of justifying one's conduct: one is the method of class logic, reasoning from a particular to a universal, or vice versa; and the other is the method of ends and means, reasoning from what is desired as an end to what is necessary as a means. It is important to note that Socrates follows the latter course. His ethical views, the background against which he interprets the state, are teleological or goal directed. He talks about justice as something desirable both as a means and as an end. One who thinks in terms of means and ends is thinking in terms of an organization or a machine, or, in the case of living things, an organism. Thus in the Socratic analysis, the city is an organized whole, comprising within itself subsidiary wholes that owe their characteristics to the way they function in the larger whole. In such a context, what is reasonable, or right, or just? Obviously, that each part perform its own function and perform it well. Reviewing the traditional virtues, Socrates has no difficulty in pointing out the special correlation between wisdom and a properly functioning intellectual elite, between courage and a properly functioning body of auxiliaries, and between temperance and a properly functioning productive class. Similar correlations are drawn between the virtues and the parts of the soul. But justice does not belong to any one part of the city or of the soul; it is the property of the whole when its parts are functioning energetically and well, not getting in each other's way.

The entire exercise of defining the virtues is something of a tour de force, the plausibility of which is hard for us, who have no feel for the traditional Greek virtues, to judge. But the exposition has a certain plausibility insofar as it concerns justice because the usual notion of justice — the one used in the courts — is that neither litigant should have what belongs to the other, and, more broadly, that everyone ought to obey the law and do what is expected of him according to his place in society. In the latter sense particularly, justice would seem to be almost equivalent to civic virtue.

We have not yet fully disposed of the original question *Why should I obey the state?* Because justice is considered desirable in itself, is obedience to the state also good in itself? If so, what is to be done in cases (such as the one Plato could never forget, in which the Athenian assembly commanded Socrates to quit teaching) in which obedience to the state conflicts with one's attempt to obey one's own reason? This is a difficult question, mainly because justice is valuable both as an end and as a means. When Socrates argues that justice is valuable as an end, he is maintaining that the individual soul is part of a universal order and that this order, which is the proper object of man's reason, is the supreme object of the soul's desire. Everywhere, order is preferable to disorder. One must desire it in one's self, in other persons, in society, and in nature. But justice is also a means, being a precondition for every other good. Thus, when an unjust ruler commands something that is contrary to the just laws of the city, the just man must disobey him, but he must do so in the way that will cause the least injustice to others. (This problem is discussed in Plato's *Apology* and *Crito*.) When injustice is endemic to a city, the wise man will disengage himself as much as he can from public affairs in order to cultivate his own virtue. In short, Socrates' moral absolutism makes him a political relativist. His justification for the state is that it nurtures morality, and for this reason, states ought to be obeyed; but the man of mature judgment has to decide for himself the limits of his duty to the state and how best to resolve any conflict between the requirements of political order and those of other kinds of order.

HISTORY

History as such does not pose a philosophical problem for Plato. Our question *Can man do without the state?* suggests to modern readers the possibility that the state is merely a transitional order and that one goal of politics should be to construct a society in which coercive authority is no longer necessary. However, to Plato it could mean only *Is it possible for man to remain a savage or to return to the savage condition after he has known civilization?* This question hardly merits an answer, although it does have the value of making explicit an assumption that we often leave unexamined, namely that civilization is a higher form of life than that which is available to the tribesman and the villager. This assumption, which also underlies the modern belief in progress, is basic to the thought of Plato, who did not believe in historical progress, although he did believe in what we might call a spiritual progress, an ascent of the individual soul from a lower to a higher condition.

Instead of talking about history, in Plato's case we must talk about metaphysics, that is to say, about his analysis of our world of materiality and change — what he calls the world of becoming — into its elements: the part which *is*, because it is always the same, and the part which *is not*, because it is never the same. The part of our existing world that remains the same (form, order) is real because it is eternal and the part of the soul by which we know it (reason) is also real. The other ingredient in our world is the opposite of real. We cannot know it, and the part of the soul that is affected by it (sensation, appetite) is correspondingly unreal. Man's existence in the world is a never-ending struggle between the higher and the lower elements within his soul. In order to exist at all, man must have some order in his life, and the level of his existence is determined by the extent to which he orders his own life using his reason. These assumptions are the foundations that underlie Plato's discussion of order, of freedom, and of justice. The city, and especially the part of the city that we call the state,(or political order), is indispensable in the progress of man's soul from a near-brutish to a near-divine condition. Thus if the question is raised whether or not man can do without the state, the answer is: Of course he can, and many men do; but without the aid of the state no man can reach the goal to which every soul aspires.

As to the progress and regress of cities, Plato has nothing decisive to say beyond the obvious fact that villages do develop into cities, that some cities are better than others, and that the best cities inevitably decline. In a particularly brilliant section of the *Republic*, Socrates traces the decline of the hypothetical best city, exhibiting the typical constitutions (timocracy, oligarchy, democracy, tyranny) of the Greek world as deformations from the ideal, each one worse than the one before it and each one owing its defects to some excess in its predecessor. This passage is not suited to encourage believers in progress or even lovers of democracy and of what we have called negative liberty, but we must not equate pessimism with belief in historical regress. Although Plato undoubtedly believed in cyclic change, an almost-universal theory among the ancients, the belief plays but little part in his political thought. Instead of orienting his city toward the past, he orients it toward eternity, where the ideal pattern lies. Even when he traces the decline of the virtuous city, his purpose is not to uncover an inevitable cyclic pattern but to disclose particular causal relations which, hopefully, can be remedied once they are brought to light. Indeed, Socrates is made to insist that his ideal city can exist, and that given a few happy circumstances, it can exist anywhere, any time. We have, then, to conclude that history does not make much difference to Plato, that what interests him is the eternal struggle of man's soul for salvation, and that although much of the success of the individual depends on the circumstances of time and place, these matters lie beyond the scope of philosophy. They are spoken of, if at all, in the language of myth, as in the conclusion of the *Republic*, which shows souls picking out their fates before plunging into the world.

In order to understand Plato, it is helpful to remember his personal interest in mathematics and his insistence that practice in abstracting mathematical forms from sensible appearances is the best preparation for philosophy, which also deals with abstract forms and patterns. Early in the *Republic*, Socrates insists on this method. If we want to understand the art of medicine, he says, we have to distinguish between what the physician does as a doctor and what he does as a businessman. The art of medicine differs from the art of making money, and particularly because the same man may practice both arts, we must learn to think about the physician's art apart from his other actions. Similarly, in order to understand the nature of the state, one must abstract its essential structure from its accidental features. Plato's playful imagination has fleshed out the abstraction so that readers (including Aristotle) have sometimes forgotten that Plato's republic is only an abstraction, not a plan for the builders of nations.

III

ARISTOTLE

The modern equivalent of the old Indian story about the blind men and the elephant concerns an international symposium on elephants. The German representative presented *An Introduction to the Study of Elephants* in three volumes; the Frenchman, a slender volume called *The Elephant and Love*; the Englishman's book was called *My Elephants, with Photographs by the Author*; and the American's contribution, which was mostly charts and graphs, bore the title *Bigger and Better Elephants*. So it is with the philosophers in writing about politics.

We have emphasized Plato's predilection for analysis. It is usually pointed out that Aristotle was greatly interested in biology and that when he took up the study of politics his work turned out to be a natural history of the state. Aristotle, who was not an Athenian by birth or rearing, resided for a number of years at the Academy and later returned to Athens to start his own school, the Lyceum. Although Aristotle remained close to Plato on fundamentals, he found fault with his teacher in detail — usually (the defender of Plato will say) because he mistook as statements of fact or as practical recommendations what Plato had intended as merely theoretical constructions. In any case, Aristotle's *Politics* is of interest as much for its observation and analysis of existing political constitutions as it is for its philosophical insights into the nature of the state and its projection of the political ideal.

Aristotelian philosophy, as distinct from Aristotelian science, came into existence when Plato's most talented pupil conceived the possibility of carrying the distinction between matter and form a step farther than his teacher had done. Plato had observed that everything has its material part and its formal part and that, in addition, some things have souls. These three aspects he was inclined to view as three separate realms of being, and his main practical interest was to find out how the soul can free itself from the realm of matter in order to participate more fully in the realm of forms. Although Aristotle was not sympathetic to Plato's transcendental outlook, he did regard Plato's teaching that things possess different degrees of reality as important for understanding nature.

In Aristotle's opinion it was a mistake to treat of matter, forms, and souls as separate entities. On the contrary, when we distinguish the matter from the form in any given thing, say a house, it turns out that what is matter in the house is something that has its own distinctive form — such as stone, brick, or lumber. Furthermore, the house itself is matter when considered in relation to such higher forms as the household or the village. Thus, neither pure matter nor pure form exists, nor do souls exist apart from matter and form, being simply the forms of living things. To call a thing matter is merely to say that it is suited to take a variety of forms, or in Aristotelian terms, that it has certain potentials that await actualization. According to Aristotle, forms constitute a natural hierarchy, from the simple elements on up to man — each kind serving as matter to the one next higher in the scale. In other words, everything in nature has a purpose or use. Because man, as a rational being, stands higher in the order of nature than rocks and plants and animals, all of them realize their purpose when he transforms them by art into something he can use. Man has no other end than to exercise his various capacities in the best possible way. But because man is naturally a social being, he can realize his capacities only in the advanced form of human association called the *polis*.

ORDER

The question whether the state is natural or artificial might draw a demurrer from Aristotle, because in his philosophy everything that is artificial is also natural. The city is just as natural as the beehive, and the main problem of the philosopher is to discover what distin-

guishes the fully organized human community from the fully organized insect community. Inasmuch as this distinction stems from
man's ability to reason, that is, from his consciousness of ends and
his ability to deliberate about the appropriateness of means to realize those ends, it becomes clear that, on Aristotle's premises, the city
is a product of art. But the basic question remains as to whether the
political order is mainly a conscious undertaking, like a business
partnership, or whether it is essentially habitual, like a family. On
this point, too, Aristotle is quite clear; but before turning to it, we
must consider what Aristotle means by the state.

Aristotle follows Plato in distinguishing between urban society
based on the division of labor, and the state considered as a political
society. The former provides the conditions necessary for the latter,
and the latter provides the order necessary for the former, but they
are not identical. Urban society embraces six different functions
(food supply, crafts, arms, finance, religion, and government), each
of which comes to be the concern of one or more distinct social
classes. Inasmuch as only two of these six functions belong to the
state (arms and government), only the two classes concerned with
these functions are, properly speaking, members of the state. In fact,
except for differences in age, the fighting and the governing classes
are identical; young male citizens make up the military class, older
male citizens constitute the governing class.

The state cannot consist of working men or of women and children because its members must have the kind of education that
enables men to judge correctly concerning practical matters and because they must be freed from other occupations in order to attend
to the business of the state. By comparison with other classes, the
members of the citizen class are both free and equal. They are free,
not merely in the sense that, unlike slaves or wage earners, they are
not obliged to take orders from their superiors, but *free* also in the
special sense which the word takes in the Greek (somewhat like our
word *liberal*) of being able to transcend mean and selfish interests
and to devote themselves to the common good. They are equal, not
in the sense that they all have the same abilities, but in the sense that
they are confreres in the arts of government and warfare.

When these matters are understood, the difference between the
state and the family becomes quite clear. The household offers no
equality and very little freedom. The husband is superior to his wife,
the father to his children, the master to his slaves. The superiority is
based in nature, lying partly in the greater strength of the adult

male, but mainly in his superior practical wisdom. For this reason the family is a different kind of association from the state, which is a partnership of persons all of whom are qualified to manage not merely their own affairs and those of their families but also those weightier affairs which pertain to the safety and prosperity of the city.

Aristotle's survey of the constitutions available to him illustrates these principles. Governments can be divided into two main classes according to whether they function as fathers or as masters. Governments worthy of the name have as their main concern the welfare of the governed, just as the father has as his main concern the welfare of his family. Whether the authority rests in one man (monarchy) or in a few (aristocracy) or in the majority (republic), it always has at heart the best interests of the city and of its citizens. However there are also governments not worthy of the name, which stand in the same relation to the governed as masters stand to slaves. The master does not, at least in his capacity as master, concern himself with the welfare of the slave, but considers only how to use the slave for his own advantage. Thus when rulers use the city for their own advantage instead of seeking its welfare, we say that the people have been enslaved, whether by one man (tyranny) or by a few men (oligarchy) or by the majority (democracy).

Strictly speaking, says Aristotle, cities that have been enslaved ought not to be called states, because a state is an association of men who are free and equal. How, then, one may ask, can a monarchy be called a state? Is the king not simply a father to his people, and is the same inequality not present in a city ruled by one man as in a family ruled by one man? This point is admitted by Aristotle, who has the task, however, of distinguishing between cities governed by benevolent monarchs and cities governed by outright despots. The reason for considering royalty a true form of government is that in this case the eminence of a man or of a family is recognized by his subjects and is embodied in their constitution. This is indirectly attested by the fact that those cities whose constitutions do not make any provision for royalty have provisions for ostracizing and banishing men of special eminence whose presence disturbs the political equilibrium.

Whether government ought to be in the hands of the many or of the few depended, in Aristotle's view, on the economic and social composition of a particular city. The men into whose hands the destiny of the city is entrusted must be concerned with the well-being of the whole city, and they must have the ability and experience necessary to give it rational direction. Although the number of men qualified to rule varies widely from city to city, Aristotle favors a compromise between government by the few and government by the many. It is well to give citizenship to all qualified persons, thus making them eligible for membership in deliberative assemblies and on trial juries, but to reserve administrative posts for those meeting special qualifications. Under this arrangement, citizens would not be equal in all points, but the fundamental principle of self-government would be preserved without losing the benefits of good government. Good government requires that decisions be made by men who understand the art of governing, that is to say, men who know what means are best suited to achieve desired ends. Because the proper end of government is the common interest, it is important that the different interests of the city be heard from on the principle that a feast to which many contribute will be richer than one which a man spreads for himself.

Let us return to the question whether the state is natural or artificial. Obviously the state involves a great deal of art, if art is understood to include the organization of human activities with a view to attaining particular goals. According to Aristotle, even the family exists to provide men with benefits that they could not get as individuals. When families unite to form villages, they do so to achieve additional goods. A similar motive prompts villages to unite to form cities, but at this level, a curious transformation occurs. Men seek a material good, usually security, when they form cities: but when men have learned to live in cities, they reap new and undreamed-of benefits. "The state comes into existence, originating in the bare needs of life, and continuing in existence for the sake of a good life."[1] In the city that is secure against marauders and well supplied with necessities, that is made comfortable and attractive by the arts, that has festivals and games to enliven man's spirit and poetry and philosophy to exercise his mind, man attains a new stature. Man has a natural reluctance to abandon his rustic habits and to learn new ways, but like every other creature, he has a built-in desire to attain the full actualization of his powers. Men naturally flourish under civilization, and thus the civilized man, rather than the savage, is the true child of nature.

That city life is natural does not make it any less a matter requiring constant and careful attention. All the classes that make up the urban society must be, in one degree or another, masters of a craft, the most important craft of all being that practiced by the citizen class, which is responsible for the city's total welfare. In the first book of the *Ethics*, Aristotle calls politics the master art. Each art, he says, has some end (as health is the end of medicine, the ship is the end of shipbuilding); but some arts are superior to or encompass other arts (as the art of riding encompasses the art of harness making, and the art of military strategy encompasses the art of riding). Politics is the art that is above all other arts; it encompasses the affairs not merely of the political class but also of the whole city by focusing on the highest good, the good for all men. Because politics is not concerned simply with the good of one man or of one family but with the good of the whole city, it is the finest and most godlike of the arts.

FREEDOM

"He who is unable to live in society," says Aristotle, "or who has no need because he is sufficient for himself, must be either a beast or a god: he is no part of a state."[2] A man cut off from his family or village or city is like a hand or foot severed from the body — he is not really a man because a thing is defined by its function and capacity, and when it is permanently incapable of exercising these, it ceases to be what it purports to be. For these reasons, Aristotle's answer to the question whether the individual is prior to the state is: "The state is by nature clearly prior to the family and to the individual, since the whole is of necessity prior to the part; for example, if the whole body be destroyed, there will be no foot or hand. . . ."[3] The practice of comparing society to a living organism has been disastrous in the history of social thought, and it is necessary to remark at once that Aristotle does not press the analogy much beyond this point. In fact, one of the criticisms Aristotle makes of his teacher is that Plato sometimes abstracts the good of society from the good of its members, as when he argues that the citizen must pursue the common good and not his own advantage. Whether Aristotle's own position is really much different from Plato's may be questioned, but the fact that he expressly refuses to subordinate the good of the citizen to that of the city shows that he does not mean to press the analogy of the body and its organs to its ultimate conclusion. He is saying that man can realize his full capacities as a rational being only as a member of a state — meaning, of course, the

Greek city-state, defined as an association of persons who are free and equal. According to Aristotle, only those men who enjoy the leisure and the refinements made possible in the city and who are fortunate enough to live under good laws and a wise constitution so that their moral and intellectual capacities are exercised in the arts of war and of government can realize the full stature of man. Although in the best city all adult males of the citizen class realize these ends, in Aristotle's sober judgment, few cities (none outside of Hellas) have circumstances that permit even men of this class to realize their stature to any high degree. However, for free men living under inferior constitutions and prevented by tyrants or by the mob from exercising their powers in government, there remains the life of contemplation, which also calls into play man's moral and intellectual powers and which opens an alternate way to self-realization.

This discussion has followed Aristotle's use of the word *free* in speaking of members of the citizen class as free men. This use accorded with the speech of that day and may be viewed as an attempt by the philosopher to give an intelligible account of the meaning of that kind of freedom popularly attributed to citizens. Such freedom is a kind of autonomy or self-sufficiency possible only to members of the human species who live in political society and, among them, attainable only by those individuals who perfect themselves in the moral virtues (thus the *Ethics* is a prolegomenon to the *Politics*) and who master the art of government. Aristotle is also familiar with another use of the word *free* — that sense in which it was employed by spokesmen for democracy who claimed freedom as the principle of the democratic constitution and who construed freedom to mean not merely the right of all men to participate in the government of the city but, more particularly, the right of everyone to do what he likes and not to be governed at all. That freedom has this second meaning, Aristotle admits; it is the kind of freedom that the slave receives when he is emancipated and that is essentially negative or anarchic until it is brought under some kind of law.

JUSTICE

Suppose the question *Why should I obey the state?* is understood in the general sense of *Why should I bother about the state?* or *Why should I take seriously my duties and privileges as a citizen?* Here Aristotle's answer would be that because "man is by nature a politi-

cal animal,"[4] to try to live apart from the state is a kind of suicide
— just as it would be suicide for a bee to try to live apart from the
hive. According to Aristotle, one simply cannot go against nature;
and when we raise any question about why we should do one thing
rather than the other, in the last analysis, we are asking what our
place in nature demands of us. Suppose the question is understood
in a more explicit sense, however, to mean *Why should I obey this
particular law or command?* Then Aristotle's answer would be: "Justice is the bond of men in states; for the administration of justice,
which is the determination of what is just, is the principle of order in
political society."[5] In other words, there can be no political order
except on the condition that all members of the state obey the laws
and commands that are legally given.

Aristotle's discussion of justice, which occurs mainly in Book
Five of the *Ethics*, is a landmark in Western thought. Setting aside
the use of the word justice as a synonym for morality in general (as
when we call a man just or upright who habitually performs his
obligations), Aristotle observes that justice stands in some circumstances for that which is equal or fairly apportioned, and in others
for that which is according to law. The former use, which Aristotle
holds to be the more fundamental, is the concern of ethics; the
latter, being merely the application of the principle of fair ap-
portionment to "free and equal persons living a common life for the
purpose of satisfying their needs,"[6] is the concern of political
philosophy.

The need to translate the principle of fairness into legal terms
arises from the tendency of rulers to act unjustly, in the sense of
taking more than their share of good things. If we go back to our
earlier distinction between the two kinds of reasoning (that which
justifies conduct in terms of the suitability of means to ends and
that which justifies it in terms of particular and universal), Aristotle
seems to be saying that when men engage to become citizens, they
bind themselves to thinking in the mode of particular and universal,
but that they do so as a means of attaining the end, fundamental
justice. Reasoning from ends to means, they come to the conclusion
that the only way for members of a state (by agreement, free and
equal) to get the fundamental justice that they all want (including a
fair determination of who shall rule and for how long) is to draw up
a set of universal rules or laws that apply to every man, to those who
govern no less than to those who are governed.

In this way, the political virtue of obedience to law proves to be the best way of implementing the moral virtue of giving to each his due. Incidentally, it also implements the virtue of prudence because the laws of the state, like the rules of any art, provide a compendium of the experience of wise men in dealing with typical problems connected with governing the city. Whether or not a particular law is in fact wise is a question of the end-means variety and can be resolved only after due deliberation, not by an individual, whether he is ruler or ruled, but by mutual consultation in legislative assemblies. The general wisdom of requiring all citizens to follow rules rather than to make judgments on the spot seems undeniable, especially when the question of wisdom is considered with the question of fairness, as well as with the well-known difficulty of perceiving what is just where one's own interests are concerned. Admittedly, law cannot cover all cases; hence, one of the provisions of a wise constitution must be for training and appointing officers to determine such matters. Still, the supremacy of the law must never be in doubt.

> Therefore he who bids the law rule may be deemed to bid God and Reason alone rule, but he who bids man rule adds an element of the beast; for desire is a wild beast, and passion perverts the minds of rulers, even when they are the best of men. The law is reason unaffected by desire.[7]

From what has been said, it is not difficult to see how Aristotle wishes to deal with the observations of the Sophists, later taken up by antipolitical groups of all sorts, who argue that what states call justice is merely conventional and has no basis in nature. Aristotle says that the laws of states are indeed conventional, and that they differ from city to city much in the way that standards of measurement do; but the variation is easily exaggerated, and one can easily see which of the laws in a particular city agree with the laws of nature and which do not. Aristotle's teaching on this point, similar to that later popularized by the Stoic philosophers and afterward taken up by Thomas Aquinas and Richard Hooker, has helped men define the notion of Natural Right so important in the development of the modern philosophy of law.

One point of interest remains to be discussed; namely, the relation between justice and equality. When justice is taken in its fundamental sense of fair portion, one has to recognize — this is an important principle in the *Ethics* — that a fair portion is not always an equal portion. In other words, we are not all equal, and what is fair to one is not fair to another. When justice is taken in its political sense to mean legality, however, inequality disappears. For these reasons, Aristotle is careful to stipulate that political justice is possible only between citizens who are equal under the law, and to distinguish between political justice and the analogous principle which applies between a father and his children or his domestics.

It will seem strange to us, although it would not have seemed so to the ancient Greek or Roman, to be told that children and wives of citizens, not to speak of working classes and slaves, are outside the law and therefore that in the legal sense, what happens to them is neither just nor unjust. The only justice or injustice applicable to them is that based on the law of nature, especially as it applies to the household. Nature which, according to Aristotle, does nothing without a purpose, has distinguished between male and female and between freemen and slaves so that each may perform one of the special functions necessary to the domestic economy. Not all women are inferior to all men — mismatches exist in which a superior woman is married to an inferior man; similarly, not all slaves are intended by nature to serve — many have been forced into slavery through the chances of war. Still, the principle remains an important one for Aristotle. The city is a highly complex entity, made possible only by the fact that nature has given men different capacities and suited them to different functions. The notion that all men are equal and that justice consists in treating all men alike seems to Aristotle a threat to civilized living, whether it is expounded by Plato, whose communism seemed to Aristotle destructive of wholesome diversity ("like harmony passing into unison, or rhythm which has been reduced to a single foot"[8]) or by champions of democracy who instigated the practice of paying honoraria to working men for attending meetings so that they could take time off their jobs to do the work proper to free men.

> For all men cling to justice of some kind, but their conceptions are imperfect and they do not express the whole idea. For example, justice is thought by them to be, and is, equality, not, however, for all, but only for equals. And inequality is thought to be, and is, justice; neither is this for all, but only for unequals. When the persons are omitted, then men judge erroneously.[9]

HISTORY

The question *Can man do without the state?* had more topical interest for Aristotle than it did for Plato because Aristotle lived to see the virtual collapse of the Greek *polis* and the rise in the West of an Oriental type of imperialism in which political authority, based on reason and consent, was replaced by a quasi-paternal authority, based on piety and obedience. The changes were profoundly unsettling to the men whose world revolved around the *polis*. The city had its last-ditch defenders, such as the orator Demosthenes. But no less conspicuous were the Cynics, a cult who gave a new twist to the Sophist distinction between natural and conventional, and who made a great show of contempt for the city and of devotion to what they chose to think of as the life of nature. Their best showman was one Diogenes, who slept in a barrel and who walked the streets in daytime with a lighted lantern looking for an honest man. In the midst of this uproar Aristotle maintained a clinical reserve. He had no sympathy with the anarchism of men like Diogenes, and his repeated insistence that the state is natural and that man is a political animal seems to be mainly directed against this movement back to nature. But neither had he any zeal for Demosthenes' lost cause, his opinion being that, at least in Athens, democracy had deteriorated into a tyranny of the worst over the best. As to Alexander's Oriental-style empire, Aristotle had nothing to say. Such empires were nothing new, having existed from time immemorial among barbarians, who are by nature incapable of self-government and must be kept in permanent tutelage to a man whom they can worship. A natural superiority enabled the Greeks to develop the state, in which free and equal men took turns governing each other. The invention of the state by the Greeks brought human powers to their highest development. But no state was ever flawless, and the true forms of government are easily perverted. When this happens, the slight advantage that the Greeks had over the barbarians disappears, and nothing remains but for them to be subjected to the will of some despot. Aristotle had served under benevolent despots (Hermias of Assos and Philip of Macedon), and he always kept open the possibility of a man or a family of men so preeminent in virtue and political ability "that all should joyfully obey such a ruler, according to what seems to be the order of nature."[10] Although this possibility existed within the framework of a constitution that made it possible for subjects to enjoy the dignity of citizens, one ought not to confuse such a state with the divine monarchies of Egypt and Mesopotamia.

For Aristotle, history makes no more sense than it does for Plato. Cities rise and fall, and although the causes are intelligible in detail (Aristotle is conscious of the influence of climate, terrain, and geography upon constitutions), no general pattern emerges. The small, face-to-face political society typical of Greek civilization is necessary for the realization of man's highest capacity, namely, rational self-determination. The main difference between Plato and Aristotle lies in the latter's reverence for nature. Plato regards the world of becoming as a mixture of the real and the unreal, and he holds that man's proper goal is to achieve deliverance from the world. Aristotle takes the world of becoming as the ultimate reality, and he sees no higher goal for man than to realize his fullest capacity as a natural being, by following either the active life of politics or the contemplative life of philosophy.

We shall see, when we consider the political philosophy of Augustine, the close affinity some Christian thinkers have for Plato. Initially, Aristotle's this-worldliness was thought to be incompatible with Christianity, but with the revival of Greek studies in the high Middle Ages, Aristotelian philosophy was combined with Christianity in a remarkable way, chiefly by Thomas Aquinas. By distinguishing between nature and grace and between reason and revelation, Aquinas found it possible to follow Aristotle very closely in matters pertaining to this world, while reserving to Scripture and the teaching of the Church those matters pertaining to the world beyond. As a result of Aquinas's influence, the most thorough-going disciples of Aristotle in the modern world are found in the Roman Catholic Church. A full account of the history of political philosophy must, therefore, include the writings of Aquinas and other medieval Aristotelians who contend that the state is a natural institution rather than a divine establishment, and who believe that it is quite safe to follow the Greek philosopher in these matters, particularly in his contention that political authority derives from the consent of the governed and that the laws of states originate in the laws of nature.[12]

IV

AUGUSTINE

No theoretical attempts to bridge the gulf between them can change the historical fact that our morality goes back to the Christian religion and our politics to the Greco-Roman conception of the state, so that they spring from different moral sources. This divided allegiance, sanctioned by custom for twenty centuries, is a necessity which modern philosophers try to convert into a virtue.

So writes Werner Jaeger in his study of Hellenic culture.[1] The perennial interest that Augustine has for Western man springs from this problem of divided loyalty. A restless youth, Augustine had tried to find guidance for his life in Cicero, in the Manichean cult, in the skepticism of the late Academy, and in Neoplatonism, while pursuing his goal of professor of rhetoric. Although his mother was a Christian, he held Christianity in contempt until, after leaving provincial Africa for Rome and Milan, he heard Christianity expounded by the learned and eloquent Ambrose. Baptized at the age of thirty-three, Augustine resigned his professorship and returned to Africa, where he was eventually made Bishop of Hippo. His *City of God* was written after the sack of Rome (A.D. 410) as a reply to those who blamed the catastrophe on the fact that Rome had forsaken her old gods and worshiped Christ in their stead. Augustine is a philosopher in the same sense in which Rousseau and Marx may be called philos-

43

ophers. He is appreciated less for his arguments, which are those of a rhetorician and homilist, than for his depth of insight into the essential weakness of the classical view of the world and man, and for his firm grasp of the intellectual principles implicit in Christian doctrine.

ORDER

One difficulty in political theory is to discover principles sufficiently comprehensive to apply to empires as well as to nations and to free cities. The kind of politics familiar to Aristotle is as remote from Augustine as the politics familiar to Thomas Jefferson is from us. About all that remained of the old notion of citizenship was that of equal protection under the law. With the decline of local autonomy and the concentration of power in the hands of the emperor and his court, the state ceased to be a mutual bond and became a foreign domination, as it had always been for the subpolitical classes − the workers and the slaves. The citizen classes, who were reduced to the level of subjects, had to obey laws which did not favor them and shared in the rewards of government only when they were willing to demean themselves and become lackeys of those in power. In this situation, politics lost all its dignity.

Plato and Aristotle had already hinted that when states fall into the hands of tyrants, philosophers had best withdraw from public life. With the coming of empire, there was nothing else to do − either for philosophers or for other civic-minded people. As a result, extra-political associations (such as mystery religions, philosophical cults) sprang up to absorb the moral and spiritual energies that had formerly been devoted to the state. The new political order could not be ignored; its presence was felt everywhere; but it was something strange and capricious, like nature and like the pagan gods which it claimed to represent. Men were thankful for its favors and patient under its burdens.

Augustine's analysis of the state takes place against this background. Christianity, broadly speaking, was one of those cults to which men turned when the civic order, with its religion and its morality, no longer sufficed. Christians had more occasion than others to think seriously about the state, in view of their flat refusal to pay it the divine honors that were demanded. No one taking into account the cruel and senseless persecution to which Christians were subjected for over two centuries would blame them had they simply regarded the state as an instrument of the devil. Their attitude toward it, however, was ambivalent.

From the beginning of Christianity, Christian teachers had laid great stress on the utility of the Roman legal and military establishment for preserving order in the world and had bidden their followers to obey the civil authority implicitly, except when they were commanded to render to Caesar the worship due only to God. Christians were convinced that the emperors were wicked men. Nevertheless, their teachers firmly maintained that God had placed authority in the hands of the civil authorities and that in obeying them, men were doing God's will. The New Testament contains two classic passages on this topic.

> Let every person be subject to the governing authorities. For there is no authority except from God, and those that exist have been instituted by God.[2]

> Be subject for the Lord's sake to every human institution, whether it be to the emperor as supreme, or to governors as sent by him to punish those who do wrong and to praise those who do right.[3]

By Augustine's time the persecutions had ceased, and the emperors had embraced Christianity. Must Christians, then, change their attitude toward the state? Should they distinguish between a pagan and a Christian empire? What, after all, is the authority that God grants to states, and what is their place in His plan for man's salvation? To answer these questions, Augustine revived the question of order.

Augustine distinguishes three different principles of order, all of which are present in the world: the natural order, which is the order that God established for creation; the human order, which is the order that fallen man tries to impose on creation; and the redemptive order, which is the order of nature restored by the work of Christ.

The three orders are intelligible only if we keep in mind certain assumptions that the Christian thinkers took over from Judaism. Strictly speaking, the Greeks had no doctrine of creation. They came closest to it in myths that spoke of a divine king or craftsman imposing order on preexisting chaos. The world as they conceived it is a compromise between divine reason and ungovernable necessity. Jews and Christians denied the existence of any necessity beyond

God's will, crediting the whole world to His wisdom, goodness, and power. Because God is good, the world is good also; hence, the order that He established for the world, which is the pure expression of His will, is right order, the only true standard by which things may be judged. When he conforms to the natural order, man subordinates his mind to eternal truth and his will to eternal right; meanwhile, other creatures are subordinate to man, whom God set as ruler over them.

Evil came into the world, not from necessity, much less from God's will, but by the choice of man, who refused to accept a subordinate position and tried to usurp the place of God. The first effect was that when man ceased to submit his understanding to divine truth, his appetites refused to submit to his understanding. The second effect of man's rebellion was that having thrown off allegiance to God, every man was at war with every other. The third effect was that the lower creatures, as if sensing man's rebellion against their Maker, threw off his dominion over them. No creature can successfully rebel against a Creator to whom he owes his very life's breath. Man lives and thinks by virtue of the order of nature against which he tries to rebel. His erroneous thoughts and his unjust deeds can, for this reason, never be anything more than a distortion of nature. What we call the human order is simply the natural order weakened and perverted by man's pride and greed. God tolerates it in view of His purpose to redeem a portion of mankind from their fallen condition and to restore the divine order in them. This third order shares the imperfections of the human order for the present, but it is intelligible only as a work of re-creation in which the divine order is established in men's hearts, in their relations to their fellows, and ultimately throughout the whole world.

The state, according to Augustine, is the ultimate expression of the human order. Compared with the natural order, it is unjust. But insofar as it provides a framework within which men can live and work and rear children and pursue worthwhile goals, it deserves the loyalty and obedience of all men. Without some kind of order, the human species could not survive.

Augustine finds two principles at work in the state. The first is what modern men have learned to call the will to power. Augustine's term for it is *dominandi libido* — the lust of rule. According to the natural order, man is supposed to exercise rule or dominion over the lower creatures, but not over his fellowman. The desire for glory and dominion is an elementary manifestation of man's wish to usurp the place of God. Rome, which was Augustine's main concern, furnishes many examples.

> Glory they most ardently loved: for it they wished to live, for it they did not hesitate to die. Every other desire was repressed by the strength of their passion for that one thing. At length their country itself, because it seemed inglorious to serve, but glorious to rule and to command, they first earnestly desired to be free, and then to be mistress.[4]

The love of glory is somewhat higher in Augustine's opinion than the love of domination. Those who love glory must consider the opinion of others and therefore exercise some restraint.

> He who is a despiser of glory, but is greedy of domination, exceeds the beasts in the vices of cruelty and luxuriousness. Such, indeed, were certain of the Romans, who, wanting the love of esteem, wanted not the thirst for domination; and that there were many such, history testifies.[5]

A second principle, in addition to love of sovereignty, is necessary to explain the state — the desire for peace. Such a desire springs, not from man's rebellious will, like the lust for rule, but from his creaturely nature, which was made to be at harmony with itself and with the world and which can never be satisfied in the midst of turmoil and strife. According to Augustine, the disturbance that man is able to introduce into the world does not reach very deeply into the order of creation. "Even what is perverted must of necessity be in harmony with, and in dependence on, and in some part of the order of things, for otherwise it would have no existence at all."[6] Imagine, for example, a man crucified head down. Although the order of nature is violently disturbed, a kind of peace remains in the body as long as its members keep together; and even when life departs and decay enters in, the bodily elements follow an appointed order. "Throughout this process the laws of the high Creator and Governor are strictly observed, for it is by Him the peace of the universe is administered."[7] And what is true of physical processes is also true in human affairs. Peace is never far from men's minds. Even the man who lives by violence must keep peace among his followers and in his own house. Augustine smiles at the thought of a robber chief quieting his children so that he can get some rest. By making a storm, he creates a calm.

For he sees that peace cannot be maintained unless all the members of the same domestic circle be subject to one head, such as he himself is in his own house. And therefore if a city or nation offered to submit itself to him, to serve him in the same style as he had made his household serve him, he would no longer lurk in a brigand's hiding-places, but lift up his head in open day as a king, though the same covetousness and wickedness should remain in him.[8]

Taken together, the two principles of the love of rule and the desire for peace enable us to understand the political order.

It is thus that pride in its perversity apes God. It abhors equality with other men under Him; but instead of His rule it seeks to impose a rule of its own upon its equals. It abhors, that is to say, the just peace of God, and loves its own unjust peace; but it cannot help loving peace of one kind or another. For there is no vice so clean contrary to nature that it obliterates even the faintest traces of nature.[9]

If we put to Augustine the question whether the state is natural or artificial, his answer will depend on whether we consider the ruler, who lusts after glory and domination, or the ruled, who desire only peace. Concerning the ruler, Augustine's answer has to be that the state is artificial — and not simply in the sense that to rule belongs to the human order, rather than to the natural order according to Augustine's special use of the word *natural*. The state is artificial because it is an instrument of human purpose. We asked whether the state is more like a family or more like a business organization. For the ruler, it is closer to the latter — to be specific, more like organized crime. Apart from the fact that we recognize states as legitimate, their whole organizational pattern is identical with that of a robber band.

For what are robberies themselves, but little kingdoms? The band itself is made up of men; it is ruled by the authority of a prince, it is knit together by the pact of the confederacy; the booty is divided by the law agreed on.[10]

Moreover, it is entirely conceivable that, when the government of a land is derelict, a vigorous chieftain may take over a whole country and establish himself as the legitimate authority. To do this, he would need to alter neither his methods nor his goals, but only to secure his hold on places and to accustom the inhabitants to obey his commands. Augustine is not saying that rulers are particularly vicious men. He is saying that we cannot understand the nature of politics unless we recognize that men who make up the ruling body have different interests from those of their subjects. Men seek political power as an end in itself. They learn, however, that ruling is an art, and that it is difficult to remain in power without meeting their subjects' demand for peace.

The exercise of political power has another side, however, because ruling men is different from managing a zoo or even a prison. Rulers must have the consent of their subjects, which is the point of saying that states are legitimate while robber bands are not. In the Roman Empire, the people had no choice in who their rulers would be; nevertheless, every man could choose whether he would or would not be a loyal subject. The fact that a vast population, not only in Italy but in all the lands that she had conquered, quietly accepted the authority of the Caesars is a reminder that when the will to power on the part of a few is able to satisfy the desire for peace on the part of the many, the most important conditions for legitimacy have been fulfilled. From the viewpoint of the ruled, therefore, the state is less like a business organization than it is like a family. Most members of the state are content to be as ignorant of the affairs of government as children are of household management. What they mainly need to know is what is expected of them and what they can expect of others. Tradition has a great hold on the subject masses: they cherish their little privileges, and they expect certain decencies of those in power. A ruler who is scrupulous in observing traditional privileges and who is able to command obedience will be considered legitimate.

FREEDOM

The notion of political freedom seems to have held no attraction for Augustine. The good that the state can achieve he calls *peace*, understanding by that term the order that fallen man is able to impose upon human affairs by means of the essentially unjust domination that some men exercise over others. The slave, and to a great extent the subject of the state, is the loser in the struggle for domination. They have given up their freedom in exchange for their lives or for peace. According to Augustine, to exchange freedom on this basis is always a wise move, for what men commonly think of as freedom is an illusion, being merely the negative expression of that desire to be God that led to man's fall. The fact is that when slaves and subjects think that they want only to be free, what they really want is to rule; only when they learn that they cannot rule will they sue for peace. Although Rousseau and others would later say that men give up one kind of freedom to get another and better kind, Augustine does not talk this way. He sees the freedom of independence as an illusion of fallen man; the freedom that the state makes possible he prefers to call peace.

Outside the political context, Augustine has a great deal to say about freedom — about the freedom that man lost when he fell from the natural order, and about the freedom that he regains when he is received into the order of redemption. One may observe that Augustine joins Plato and Aristotle in giving a positive connotation to freedom. The free man is one whose life is regulated by the True and the Good, and not one who follows his dominant passion. But whereas those philosophers saw it as a function of the state to nurture men in the ways of freedom, Augustine believes that this is the work of Christ through his church.

The problem of political freedom, as it presents itself to political theorists, is partly a question of fact and partly a question of value. Is the individual so completely a product of society (specifically of political society) that his only freedom consists in doing willingly what society has determined he is to do? If he is not, is it important that the individual be permitted to do what he wants without the interference of society and of other men? Augustine's answer to both of these questions is no. Is the state prior to the individual? Again he would answer no. The relationship between the individual and the state is peripheral. Freedom is an affair between man and God.

JUSTICE

From what has been said about order and freedom, it is not difficult to guess how Augustine would answer the question *Why ought I to obey the state?* His answer would be *For the sake of peace.* Fallen men ought to obey the state because the order that it establishes makes it possible for them to pursue their private ends. The Bishop of Hippo knew the value of peace, as his *Confessions* show. As a provincial youth whose working class father sacrificed to give him the best schooling, Augustine won a top appointment in open competition at Rome with nothing to help him but his own talent, hard work, and determination. Shortly thereafter he became disenchanted and turned elsewhere to find happiness, but the experience left him with a deep appreciation of the advantages of a wise and stable political and social order for the private individual. In Augustine's view, redeemed man no longer pursues ambition and pleasure, in contrast to his former, sinful self. Still, as a pilgrim of the eternal sojourning in the realm of time, he cannot be indifferent to the benefits of peace, which he recognizes as part of God's providence, a provisional order, a kind of scaffolding for use while the redemptive order is being completed.

Augustine's most explicit treatment of the problem of political justice comes in connection with his discussion of Cicero's definition of a republic. Cicero points out that in order to understand the meaning of *res publica,* one must first understand the meaning of *populus* (people).

> A commonwealth is the property of a people (*res publica res populi*). But a people is not any collection of human beings brought together in any sort of way, but an assemblage of people in large numbers associated in an agreement with respect to justice and a partnership for the common good.[11]

Cicero himself mentions the difficulty posed by the presence of justice in the definition, for it might suggest that the Roman people were not always a people. In view of his doctrine of man's fall, Augustine presses this objection even further, arguing that an order based on the domination of some men by others can never be just. He therefore proposes an alternate definition.

> But if we discard this definition of a people, and, assuming another, say that a people is an assemblage of reasonable beings bound together by a common agreement as to the objects of their love, then, in order to discover the character of any people, we have only to observe what they love.[12]

This definition is broad enough to remove any question of whether the Romans were a people and their state a republic, and it can be applied to small city-states as well as to large nations and empires. Moreover, it can comprehend at once the lust of the rulers for dominion and the desire of the people for peace, because while there is but slight community of interest between these two, the two interests frequently coincide.

Because Augustine omits justice from his definition, scholars have sometimes accused him of political immoralism like that expressed by Plato's Thrasymachus, who argued that justice is whatever is to the interest of the strongest party. However, we must not base our judgment on the presence or absence of a highly emotive word. Our study of Aristotle should be sufficient to remind us that *justice* is an ambiguous term. In Cicero's account, the meaning is not entirely clear. Did he mean by the term fairness or legality? If he meant the latter, namely, that a people submits to a body of positive law, then Augustine need have no quarrel with him. If he meant the former, namely, that what people want when they bind themselves by law is to keep men from taking unfair advantage of each other, then what he calls *justice* is what Augustine calls *peace*. Aristotle, we may recall, uses the term in both ways. But Aristotle also talks about natural justice as an ideal which civic justice ought to approximate; and what Cicero seems to be saying is that only an assemblage of men who respect this higher justice is properly *a people*. However, according to Augustine, justice is never realized in the human order, represented by the state, but only in the redemptive order, represented by the church.

This seems to be the nub of the controversy between Augustine and Cicero. The pagan view of natural justice made room for glory and ambition. Men like Aristotle and Cicero had no difficulty picturing a just society in which wise and virtuous rulers accepted the gratitude and obedience of their humble and loyal subjects. Despite the charm of this ideal, however, in the Christian view it does not represent the order of nature, where every man is the equal of every other and only God is honored and obeyed. This criticism does not mean that Augustine made no distinction between good and bad rulers or between worthy and unworthy subjects. He recounts the long line of Roman heroes, whose patriotic deeds set examples of virtue, and he contrasts them with men like Nero, who had no sense of shame. Moreover, he holds up a portrait of a Christian prince — a man who realizes the vanity of glory and domination and who longs for heaven, whose subjects, meanwhile, both pagan and Christian, have cause to rejoice in his moderation and benevolence.[13] All of this testifies to Augustine's belief that fallen man retains impressions of natural truth and justice. But he also holds that within the framework of the human order, an order based on inequality and selfish ambition, true justice cannot be found.

We conclude that, like Plato and Aristotle, Augustine justifies the state by the logic of ends and means, rather than by the logic of universals and particulars. Dominion and law are instruments of civic peace; civic peace is desirable, not merely for itself, but as a necessary condition for reaching other goods, whether temporal or eternal. When Christians said that by obeying the rulers of this world men were obeying God, they must not be taken to mean that the commands of rulers are rough approximations of the commands of God, because they may or they may not be. Nevertheless, civil commands are to be obeyed, except where they infringe upon the Christian's witness and worship, because in God's providence earthly dominion, even when exercised by one as vicious as Nero, is an instrument of peace.

HISTORY

The political philosopher is interested in the concept of history only insofar as men's beliefs about meaning in history enter into their concept of the nature and function of states. Plato and Aristotle were not inclined to pay serious attention to history because the Greeks had little tendency to read any meaning into the rise and fall of states beyond that of generation and corruption, which to them seemed to characterize everything governed by time. Augustine took a different position. In the first place, Romans from the time of Virgil had cherished the notion that the empire of the Caesars would last forever and preserve peace in the world. In the second place, Jews from the time of Abraham had maintained that they were a people chosen by God to carry redemption to the world and that in the last days God would set up his throne in Jerusalem and rule all nations. What is sometimes called Augustine's philosophy of history is the attempt of a Christian to mark out a path between these two claims.

In the early days of the church, Christians were persecuted by both Romans and Jews — by the former because they refused to recognize the divinity of Caesar, by the latter because they refused to recognize the exclusiveness of Jewish national claims. Nevertheless, because the Christians held Jesus to be the hoped-for Jewish Messiah through whom God would at last rule the world, they had to explain the sense in which Jesus was a king and how his kingdom fitted in with the claims of both Romans and Jews. The early church held two main views on the subject. One was that Christ's kingdom is not of this world, that when Christ returns in glory the world as men know it will come to an end, and that after a general judgment Christ will reign over his saints in heaven. The other view was that although Christ's kingdom is of this world, it will begin only when Christ returns in glory and overcomes the nations of the world by supernatural means, after which he and his saints will rule the earth for a thousand years (the millennium mentioned in *Revelation*). The early church never entertained the thought that some day the emperors would become Christians and would try to unite the Empire and the church. When this happened, Roman Christians began to entertain a third view of Christ's reign. As Rome's claims to be eternal mingled in their minds with Israel's claims to be the bearer of redemption to fallen man, they tended to make Christianity a political religion, like Judaism, only on a vastly larger scale. Caesar became in their minds a sort of Christian David, and his throne the throne of Christ.

Of these three positions, Augustine holds to the first. He does not share the enthusiasm of the millenarians for setting dates and reading the signs of the times. He believes that, so far as God's plan of salvation is concerned, the world is in its last phase: nothing of significance remains for believers to look forward to except the return of Christ and the end of time. Some Christian writers were inclined to see a regression in the history of heathen nations. A favorite text was the account in *Daniel* of the great image with a head of gold, shoulders of silver, belly of brass, legs of iron, and feet of clay, which was ground to powder by a little stone that fell from heaven and that later became a great mountain. According to a common interpretation, Babylon was the head of gold, Persia the shoulders of silver, Macedon the belly of brass, and Rome the legs of iron. The little stone was God's Anointed who, at His return, would destroy the whole heathen system and establish His kingdom in its place. Although Christians had long identified Rome with the last stage of heathen rule, Augustine ignores this view. For him, the recent sack of Rome is not a sign of the end of the world and a cause for Christians to rejoice. On the other hand, it is no cause for Christians to lament either, inasmuch as the fate of empires is to be overthrown.

Augustine's so-called philosophy of history is an attempt to place contemporary events in a divine perspective. One cannot rightly call his view a philosophy because Augustine does not profess to know anything about history that is not revealed in the pages of God's word. Augustine's contribution might be called a theology of history, but it is hardly even that because the only part of history that has meaning for the authors of Scripture, and thus for Augustine, is that which leads from Adam to Christ and traces the stages of God's redemptive work. To be sure, Scripture recognizes two lines of development — that of the children of this world, represented by Cain, the first murderer and a builder of cities; and that of the children of God, represented by Abel, the first martyr, a pilgrim, and a stranger in the world. Augustine envisages two great companies, each comprising angels as well as men, including the deceased and the unborn as well as the living. These companies, he says, may be called Cities, in a mystical sense. Each is identified by its distinctive love: the Earthly City by love of self; the Heavenly City by love of God. Throughout history the two Cities have mingled here on earth: God has his saints in the household of Caesar, while Satan has his Judases in the household of Christ. The love of self and of this world is the bond of cities and states, even as the love of God is the force that leads men to forsake cities and binds them together into churches. Events in the world, such as the sack of Rome, can be understood by Christians only if they keep in mind the two mystical Cities. Kingdoms and empires rise and fall in monotonous succession. God uses them in his providence, but that providence is known only to Him.

We must conclude that, although the problem of history faced him in a way in which it did not face Plato and Aristotle, Augustine refused to take it seriously. We might even say that, as far as secular history is concerned, Augustine is a positivist and agnostic, and that he agrees with those in our time who insist that anyone who claims to know what history holds for man must be an inspired prophet. As far as he is concerned, divine inspiration traces the history of the Heavenly City through New Testament times, but beyond that it is silent. Jesus told His disciples that no man knows the time or season of His coming again. Augustine found nothing in Scripture that would have enabled men to predict the conversion of the Roman emperors, nor did Scripture reveal anything to him about what the future held for Rome. Augustine had opinions, like any other man: he was optimistic with respect to Rome's recovery, and he was not sure that persecution of Christians might not be resumed. But these were no more than opinions.

We have suggested that not all Christian thinkers are as reticent about history as Augustine was. If they were, we would not be compelled to treat the problem of history as a main concern of political philosophy. It is mainly the Christian influence on Western thought that has encouraged men to think that states have the responsibility for promoting the kingdom of God (or its equivalent) on earth. All Christians believe that they are obliged to follow an ethic of perfection and that they have to distinguish, as Augustine did, between this ethic and the ethic of accommodation and expediency prevailing in business and in politics. But some Christians understand from Scripture that the ethic of perfection is to replace the ethic of accommodation in the forum and in the marketplace. Some of them try to set up miniature kingdoms of Christ, governed by divine law, in the midst of or alongside of the kingdoms of the world. Some identify the kingdom of Christ with a particular nation and, attaching God's laws to it, try to use it to fight His battles. Some see themselves as the heralds of Christ's immanent return, commissioned to line up the faithful against the powers of unrighteousness which Christ is shortly to destroy. These are complications that the Greeks did not have to face because their Heavenly City had no connection with time. Augustine refuses to face them because his Heavenly City is only a sojourner in time. The problem of history arises when men affirm that God intends to establish His City in the world and that, sooner or later, all the cities of the world must come to terms with it.

V

HOBBES

Thomas Hobbes is the first of the long line of thinkers who have tried to construct a science of human conduct after the pattern of Galileo's science of matter in motion. All science (or philosophy), Hobbes said, consists in reasoning from effects to causes or from causes to effects. In other words, one proceeds scientifically either when he begins with something he wants to understand and resolves it into elements which he already knows, or when he begins with known elements and constructs something from them. The method was first developed by geometers. For example, a square can be resolved into straight lines, equal angles, and so forth; or it can be constructed from these parts. Galileo applies this method to mechanics in studying the motions of a pendulum or of a projectile. Hobbes applies the method to the body politic. Take any question arising in political discourse, say the justice or injustice of an act. Upon analysis, the notion of justice resolves into that of legality; but a thing is legal when it is commanded by one who has coercive power. Power, in turn, reduces to the wills of men; and men's wills are composed of appetite and deliberation. Hence, we come at last to the elements on which the state is built — appetite and reason. Using the synthetic method, we are led from a consideration of man's appetites and his capacity for making choices to the point where men find it necessary to submit their wills to a sovereign power whose commands give rise to the distinction between just and unjust.

Hobbes had more than a theoretical interest in finding a scientific basis for politics. He lived through the period of civil war when the armies of Parliament had defeated those of the King and the King had been beheaded. In Hobbes's opinion, the main cause of these unhappy events was the failure of the people to understand the nature of the state. In the absence of a definitive science of politics, Catholics and Protestants, Anglicans and Presbyterians filled the air with their unfounded opinions and led people astray. What the land wanted, in Hobbes's opinion, was a king who would be sufficiently philosophical to recognize the validity of the new science and sufficiently astute to make sure that it was widely understood.

ORDER

Hobbes is the kind of philosopher who has a clear and definite answer to almost any question, due mainly to the importance that, following the geometrical method, he attaches to definitions. He will tell us quickly enough what liberty and justice are, and he has a plain and intelligible answer to our question as to whether the state is natural or artificial.

> Nature, the art whereby God hath made and governs the world, is by the art of man, as in many other things, so in this also imitated, that it can make an artificial animal.[1]

This animal (Hobbes's Leviathan) is the commonwealth or state, which he calls an artificial man because when a body of men is represented by one man or a designated body of men, the multitude becomes a person with a single will and purpose. Hobbes argues that the construction of states is analogous to the construction of houses and other buildings. Long before men knew anything about the science of physics, they used the principles of physics in building, but now the new scientific knowledge makes it possible for them to build better and more lastingly. In a similar manner, political society has always used the principle of a sovereign body owing its authority to the allegiance of great numbers of people, but in the past the failure to understand that principle and all that it implies has led to political instability, which the new science of politics should help men to eliminate.

The keystone of the state, according to Hobbes, is the contract whereby a multitude of men resign their rights to some man or group of men who henceforth will have sovereign rights over them all. The contract theory of the state was not in itself a new one, having been put forward by the ancient Sophists. Glaucon mentions it in the *Republic* as the theory of men who, disliking to practice justice but disliking more to suffer injustice, enter into a contract whereby all agree to abide by common rules. The weakness in this theory, as Glaucon himself recognizes, is that a person who does not value justice for its own sake will enter into a contract readily enough, but he will violate it whenever such action seems more to his advantage. In order to explain the existence of states, the contract must be something more than a mutual agreement to act justly. States are effective in protecting men from injustice because they are authorized agents that bring the force of the entire community to bear against anyone who is inclined to act unjustly. A contract must exist, either explicitly or implicitly, between every member of the community and every other member, but the substance of the contract is not simply an agreement to act justly as long as others do the same; rather it is an agreement to surrender to a sovereign person control over all one's affairs.

> And in him consisteth the essence of the commonwealth; which, to define it, is one person, of whose acts a great multitude, by mutual covenants one with another, have made themselves every one the author, to the end he may use the strength and means of them all, as he shall think expedient, for their peace and common defence.[2]

By this act of surrender, men bring the state into existence. What was formerly a mere aggregation becomes now a public person.

A truly natural society, according to Hobbes, would resemble that of the bees or the ants, which live together peaceably without any covenant and without any government. Such a society is not possible among men, chiefly because of man's ability to reason. Like other living things, man always acts in order to satisfy some desire, but by virtue of his exceptional powers of thought, he has a peculiarly troublesome set of desires to satisfy. He is not content when his bodily appetites are satisfied because he is worried about their future satisfaction, and in this way he develops an appetite for power, which takes such oblique forms as desire for glory. Men are, therefore, by nature envious and distrustful. They cannot come together without each trying to best the other. Any kind of cooperative effort is soon weakened by the desire of each man to show himself

wiser than the other, even at the cost of wrecking the whole undertaking. The insects, says Hobbes, agree with one another by nature,
but it is hard to believe that they would agree if they had the art of
speech and could vie with one another in making the worst cause
appear good and the best cause appear bad. Because men have this
capacity, any agreement among them "is by covenant only, which is
artificial."

> ... therefore it is no wonder if there be somewhat else required,
> besides covenant, to make their agreement constant and lasting;
> which is a common power to keep them in awe, and to direct
> their actions to the common benefit.[3]

Man's natural condition, in this view, is one of war. Men are by
nature so nearly equal that each man's hope of attaining the thing he
covets is strong enough to overcome any fear he may have of another's reprisal. If no supervening power exists to hold men in check,
each is determined to resort to force and treachery to get his fellows
under his power. Notwithstanding, the condition of war can never be
to men's liking. In time of war nothing is secure: agriculture, commerce, society, and the arts are all disrupted; fear of death is constant; and "the life of man, solitary, poor, nasty, brutish, and
short."[4] Man's capacity for thinking, the chief cause for strife, can
also show him the way to peace. All that is necessary is for men to
say to each other, "I authorize and give up my right of governing
myself, to this man, or to this assembly of men, on this condition,
that thou give up thy right to him, and authorize all his actions in
like manner."[5]

Hobbes's method, it must be remembered, is that of analysis and
synthesis. Hobbes, who follows Plato the mathematician rather than
Aristotle the natural historian, explicitly distinguishes between scientific knowledge, based on demonstration, and historical knowledge,
based on fact. Although he chiefly follows the former method,
Hobbes sometimes appeals to what the reader knows from introspec-
tion or from experience in the world in support of his demonstration. Hobbes's unflattering portrait of human nature is thus based
partly on his analysis of political institutions, which assumes that
force is necessary to secure the peace, and partly on his synthetic
account of nature, which attempts to explain everything by means
of elementary laws of motion. However, he thinks that the reader
will find this description is confirmed by his everyday experience

and his insight into his own conduct. The same combination of methods occurs in the account Hobbes gives of man's prepolitical condition. Hobbes arrives at his conclusion partly by way of his analysis of the state and partly by way of his account of human motivation, yet he argues that his view of the war of all against all is confirmed in reports of the New World aborigines, in the precautions that civilized men take against thieves and marauders, and in the perpetual hostility that exists between sovereign states. When Hobbes talks about men entering into contracts with each other, he does not refer to particular historical occasions as much as to the underlying assumption in all society, a contractual agreement of which men are only dimly aware until it is revealed to them by analysis.

Hobbes recognizes two main classes of commonwealth — the commonwealth in which men voluntarily give their rights over to a ruling body, and the commonwealth in which the people are forcibly subjected to the dominion of a conqueror. The second commonwealth might seem to rest on no covenant, and its subjects to remain in a condition of war. In effect, however, when men cease resisting their vanquisher, they make a convenant with him and he becomes their sovereign by the same right as that of hereditary kings or elected officials. Nor is the covenant principle limited to states. It must be by covenant, for example, that the husband exercises dominion over his wife and over their children. "A great family, if it be not part of some commonwealth, is of itself, as to the rights of sovereignty, a little monarchy."[6]

Hobbes's answer to the question whether the state is natural or artificial is that any form of human association is artificial. In some instances the common bond or interest is temporary; in other instances, permanent. Designating any group of men joined in one interest or business as a *system*, Hobbes calls the former *irregular systems* and the latter *regular systems.* A regular system is made possible by the emergence of a representative person, authorized to act for the whole membership, whether in a family, in a business corporation, in various governmental institutions, or in the state. What distinguishes the state from other regular systems is the fact that it is independent, not a part of any larger system or subject to any representative but its own. When states enter into treaties or alliances with each other, they form irregular systems at most, because when a state is conquered and obliged to submit to imperial rule, it is no longer an independent system.

FREEDOM

Hobbes's synthetic approach to politics, working from matter in motion to man as a creature of appetite and reason, shows man seeking peace and finding it in the state. His analytic approach, working back from political reality to its elements, discloses a prepolitical condition in which man acknowledged no restraint upon his own judgment as to what is good. Either way, our question whether the individual comes before society receives the same answer. Logically, the individual comes before society because society depends upon his will; and temporally the individual also comes before society, whether we are concerned with consenting adults forming families and more extended communities or with infants growing into rational adulthood within a constituted society. This prepolitical condition, in which each man is moved solely by his own desires, Hobbes calls *the state of nature*, but he also calls it *a state of liberty or freedom.* Man moves from the state of nature into the civil state, but as he does so he gives up his liberty and submits to the bondage of law.

Our purpose in asking whether the individual comes before the state is to illuminate the manner in which different philosophers deal with the problem of freedom. We have seen that the problem is particularly complex; and here we find that Hobbes, despite his relish for simplicity, is unable to avoid at least one complexity – namely, the distinction between psychological freedom and political freedom.

Hobbes says that, properly employed, the words *liberty* and *freedom* apply only to bodies (either animate or inanimate) and that they signify the absence of external impediment to motion. Thus water loses its freedom when it is confined within a vessel or between banks, and an animal loses its freedom when it is imprisoned or chained. Hobbes is particularly careful not to confuse freedom with power: one should not say that a stone is not free to move or that a sick man is not free to get out of bed, but rather that they lack the power necessary to do these things. Thus, Hobbes says, "a freeman, is he, that in those things, which by his strength and wit he is able to do, is not hindered to do what he has a will to."[7] A man's will is determined by many things, including his education, but this does not alter his freedom. Hobbes would apparently deny that in a technological utopia man loses any freedom so long as he is able to do what he wants to do. Even when he is restrained from a particular course of action by conscious fear of what another person may do to him, he is nonetheless free because he follows his will, and will is, by definition, "the last appetite in deliberating."[8] Psychologically, therefore, no loss of freedom occurs when man enters civil society and submits to the rule of another. On the contrary, the state owes its origin and its continued existence to the will of the subjects, who consent to have a sovereign over them. Psychologically, man is neither more nor less free in the civil state than in the natural condition.

But as important as psychological freedom is for an understanding of states, men usually have another kind of freedom or liberty in mind when they talk about political matters. This is the freedom of independence or of self-government, the kind of freedom that we have called anarchy. Political freedom is, therefore, a negative concept, being intelligible only against the background of government and law. In the state of nature, men enjoy this freedom without being aware that they have it. In the civil state they are aware of it, mainly as something that they no longer have, but also as something remaining to them in an abridged form under law. This civil or political freedom consists in those liberties that sovereigns do not find necessary to take away from their subjects. Laws, says Hobbes, are artificial chains with which men allow themselves to be bound. Unlike chains of iron, which men would break if they could, these chains can be broken by anyone who chooses. They do not take away man's elementary freedom to move as he wills, but they do bind him and take away his freedom of independence. Man creates an artificial body, the commonwealth, for the purpose of securing peace; and having voluntarily resigned his natural independence for the privilege of membership in an orderly society, he is fairly said to have given up his liberty.

By a bold stroke, Hobbes identifies liberties with rights. From Roman times, Western thinkers were accustomed to speak of natural right (*jus naturale*) and the law of nature (*lex naturalis*). In an effort to reduce political thinking to a science, Hobbes attempts to bring the legal language into harmony with his terminology. A natural right, he says, is the freedom man has to do whatever seems to him necessary for the preservation of his own life and estate. Outside the civil state, no restrictions are placed on a man's private judgment. Each one has a right to anything that he thinks he needs — including another man's possessions and even his life. This does not mean that a man has a right to everything that lies within his power; man's liberty toward other creatures is under the governance of reason, even as that of the lower animals is under the governance of instinct. Hobbes specifies that natural right is "the liberty each man hath, to use his own power, as he will himself, for the preservation of his own nature; that is to say, of his own life."[9] The next section will deal with the governance that reason exercises over man in the state of nature. Hobbes calls it the law of nature and contrasts it with the right of nature, although, he says, legal thinkers commonly confuse them, supposing that a man's right is somehow secured by a law that every man's reason makes known to him. Not so, says Hobbes. By definition, right and law are opposites.

> Right consisteth in liberty to do, or to forebear: whereas law determineth, and bindeth to one of them: so that law, and right, differ as much, as obligation, and liberty; which in one and the same matter are inconsistent.[10]

Law, therefore, diminishes liberty, not in the way that iron chains bind a man's body but in the way that sound reason and right judgment bind his will.

The antithesis between liberty and law carries from nature into the civil state. Laws do not, in Hobbes's view, grant or guarantee rights or liberties. Laws take them away. The only liberties left to men in the civil condition are (a) those which no rational being can part with, and (b) those which the sovereign finds no need to take away.

Hobbes concedes that there are some liberties that no rational being can agree to part with. No one would covenant to end his own life or yield himself up to death at the hands of others. It is understood, therefore, that when a man gives up to the sovereign his right of self-government, he makes exception of the right to resist an arrest that would lead to his death, the right to avoid self-incrimination, and the right to refuse military service. Hobbes does not concede, however, that because a citizen has a right to protect his life the sovereign is bound to respect that right. The sovereign, according to Hobbes, has only one responsibility toward his subjects; namely, to keep the peace. If he finds that he must imprison or kill men in order to do this, they have no recourse because by the contract each man gives the sovereign the right to kill him if that is necessary to preserve peace. Moreover, each citizen agrees not to resist the sovereign when he takes the life of other citizens. Still, for whatever it is worth, the individual is not bound by the covenant either to take his own life or to offer no resistance when his life is threatened by the sovereign.

Aside from these inalienable rights, the only rights of subjects are those left to them by the discretion of the sovereign: such rights as the liberty to travel, to buy and sell, to live where they like, or to bring up children as they think fit. Political society is an invention enabling men to do those things which in the state of nature they had the right or liberty to do, while lacking the power to do them. By giving up all their liberties to the state, men are, for the first time, able to avail themselves of those liberties that the state finds no need to abridge. Inasmuch as the main obstacle to peace is each man's right to decide for himself what he must do to preserve his life, that is the chief right each man must surrender when he becomes a subject of the state.

The sovereign himself remains, as it were, in the state of nature: he is bound by no law except his own good understanding and sound reason. Attempts to limit sovereignty by laws or by division are unintelligent and dangerous. They are unintelligent because anyone who understands what it is to be subject to political authority knows that someone, either a king or an assembly of men, must make decisions and see that they are enforced. In a democracy, the sovereignty is just as absolute as it is in a monarchy; and where laws are supposed to be over the sovereign, someone must interpret and apply the laws. There is no escaping the fact that, when they enter into civil society, men give up whatever liberty the sovereign finds it necessary to take away. Besides being unintelligent, it is dangerous to think that the sovereign can be limited. Attempts to limit the sovereign can have only one effect; namely, to reduce men to the natural condition that the civil order was meant to remedy. The refusal of the English Parliament to vote the taxes that King Charles required, together with the civil disturbances that followed, seems to Hobbes an unhappy confirmation of this truth.

Hobbes maintains that much of the enthusiasm for political liberty in his time stemmed from a misunderstanding of Greek and Roman authors. What the ancients prized under the name of *liberty* was not the liberty of each person to do as he pleased, but the independence of their cities from foreign domination. The public persons known as states remain free because they remain in a state of nature: they are ever at war (or in a state of armed truce) with every other nation. To say that Athenians or Romans were free men is merely to say that their states were successful in defending themselves against other states — and their success usually meant depriving other states of their liberty. To mistake this public liberty for the liberty of private men is an elementary confusion. Citizens have liberty — no one could endure life without it — but they do not have as much of it as they would like to have, and rather than increase their liberty, the city diminishes it. Moreover, the best city is not the one that diminishes liberty the least, but the one that diminishes it only at those places where liberty is most detrimental to security and peace. For example, a good state will restrict freedom of speech in the interest of preventing riots and wars.

JUSTICE

We can approach the question *Why should I obey the state?* by returning to the exception already noted; namely, the special set of circumstances in which a man is justified in disobeying the state. Students sometimes get unduly excited when they read in Hobbes that man has a right to resist the state when it threatens him bodily harm, for they suppose that Hobbes intends this right to be some kind of guarantee against oppressive measures on the part of the state. Nothing of the sort is intended. The man who resists the state becomes an outlaw, reverting to the condition of nature, and his hopes of resisting the state are never very good if the state is what it should be. Hobbes intends to emphasize the theoretical point that when a man covenants to hand over his rights to the state in order to procure peace, he cannot be understood to hand over his right to self-preservation. Therefore, if he resists an attempt by the state on his life, he is not guilty of going back on his word; he has not violated his covenant, nor is he doing anything inconsistent, unreasonable, or unjust. But — and this is the only reason for returning to the point — he would be acting inconsistently, unreasonably, and unjustly if he refused to obey the state under any other circumstances. Man enters the state because life is intolerable where there is no sovereign authority. Reason led him to see the necessity for yielding his rights to the state in the first place, and the same kind of thinking binds him at all times to obey the state. This reasoning, it may be noted, is of the kind we have called reasoning from end to means. Man desires peace, and submission to the state is the means to get it.

The just man in the primary sense, according to Hobbes, is the far-sighted man, who knows what is good for him and understands the conditions necessary to obtain it. He is also the disciplined man, who is master of his own soul. Hobbes is far from thinking that all members of the state are this rational. A coercive authority is needed precisely because most men, at the critical moment, cannot be trusted to follow reason. A majority of members of the state obey its commands, not because they see the rationality of them, but because they are afraid of being punished. Hobbes insists that these men are not just; a man who obeys a law from fear of punishment or for hope of reward is guiltless, but he is not just. Hobbes, rather like Nietzsche at this point, disdains a petty concern for personal advantage and suggests that the just man takes a reckless pride in following the impersonal demands of reason.

> That which gives to human actions the relish of justice, is a certain nobleness or gallantness of courage, rarely found, by which a man scorns to be beholden for the contentment of his life, to fraud, or breach of promise. This justice of the manners, is that which is meant, where justice is called a virtue; and injustice a vice.[11]

As Hobbes defines the term, *justice* is the keeping of covenants. But Hobbes also discusses justice in connection with law. An act is just when it conforms to law, regardless of whether the man who performs it is a just man. Moreover, there are two kinds of law: civil, and natural.

Usually, when we call an act just, we mean that it conforms to the civil law, that is, to the laws or commands of the sovereign. A good example of such a law is that which establishes the ownership of property. According to Hobbes, no property (no mine and thine) exists in the state of nature, where everyone has a right to everything. Only when a person surrenders his rights to the common sovereign and receives a title from him to specific lands or other goods can he be said to have any property. The old saying that justice is giving to each his due has no meaning outside the civil state or apart from positive laws that states lay down governing the acquisition and exchange of material goods. Obviously, then, what we ordinarily mean by justice does not exist in the state of nature. As the old Sophists were accustomed to say, justice is conventional. The point is one that Hobbes wants to emphasize. There is, he says, no possibility of going behind the positive laws of nations and claiming some prior right to one's goods. Specifically, no ground exists for the claim, which Hobbes thinks has been largely responsible for civil wars, that citizens have a right to refuse the king what he demands in taxes and troop levies. Property is a civil institution, as is the justice that respects property rights, but the king is bound by no such laws. Hobbes is not content to stop with this point, however.

Although it is true that no property rights exist in the state of nature, it would be wrong to think that no foundation for property rights (and other civil laws) exists in the state of nature. Hobbes's argument is that in the state of nature the necessity for civil laws is already apparent to reasonable men, and he includes that necessity in what he calls the law of nature. We have already discussed the law of nature as the impediment that reason raises against natural liberty. In order to get out of the state of war and to attain peace and security, man must do certain things. These conditions are the laws of nature; they are not opposed to civil laws. The contrary is the case.

> Obedience to the civil law is part also of the law of nature. Civil, and natural law are not different kinds, but different parts of law; whereof one part being written, is called civil, the other unwritten, natural. But the right of nature, that is, the natural liberty of man, may by the civil law be abridged, and restrained: nay, the end of making laws, is no other, but such restraint; without the which there cannot possibly be any peace. And law was brought into the world for nothing else, but to limit the natural liberty of particular men, in such manner, as they might not hurt, but assist one another, and join together against a common enemy.[12]

Hobbes's treatment of natural law is quite detailed. He enumerates nineteen different laws that disclose themselves to reason like so many theorems in geometry. Of these laws, the first two are more like axioms than they are like theorems. We encountered them earlier when we were considering the basis for the political order. The first law of nature has two parts: that a man ought to seek peace as long as there is any hope of obtaining it and that when there is no longer any hope he ought to avail himself of all the means necessary to wage successful war. The second law of nature is that a man be willing to lay down his rights to defend himself as long as others are willing to do likewise. Given these two laws of nature and no others, the man who is capable of following reason will know that he is obliged to obey civil laws — that is to say, the commands laid down by a sovereign — and he will see the truth of the claim that "obedience to the civil law is part also of the law of nature." The third law of nature concerns keeping covenants and specifically gives rise to justice.

From that law of nature, by which we are obliged to transfer to another, such rights, as being retained, hinder the peace of mankind, there followeth a third; which is this, that men perform their covenants made: without which, covenants are vain, and but empty words; and the right of all men to all things remaining, we are still in the condition of war.[13]

The remaining laws of nature need not be given in detail. They merely spell out those qualities of human decency that must be present to supplement mere legality and force if men are to achieve peace and contentment in states. Men must restrain their passions and their desire for glory, and they must cultivate the social virtues — gratitude, humility, clemency, and fair play. In the natural condition these virtues are worthless — force and fraud are virtues there. Hobbes says that while man remains in the state of nature, natural laws bind only his conscience, not his actions. When he enters the civil state, natural laws bind both his thoughts and his deeds; and they bind sovereign heads of states no less than subjects. For, although kings and members of elective governments are not liable to prosecution when they violate civil laws, men do not hesitate to reprobate them for violating the laws of nature, that is to say, the laws of reason. Moreover, because the laws of reason are also the laws of sound religion, men who sin against them are guilty in the eyes of God, as appears from the Biblical example of King David, who committed adultery with Bathsheba and arranged to have her husband killed. When David repented afterwards, he did so to God. "Against thee only have I sinned, and done this evil in thy sight." A monarch is bound by no law except God's law or, what is the same thing, the law of nature.

Students of Hobbes do not agree as to just how Hobbes thought the laws of nature oblige men's conscience. Conscience is moral reason; but do the laws of nature bind reason by the logic of ends and means, or by the logic of universal and particulars? Hobbes seems to think that they bind in both ways. They are necessary conditions or means for making peace.

These are the laws of nature, dictating peace, for a means of the conservation of men in multitudes; and which only concern the doctrine of civil society.[14]

Thus, the laws of nature bind each man insofar as he seeks what is good for him. But several times Hobbes mentions that such laws bind in another way as well. From his reason a man understands that every other man has the same rights as he, and that society is possible only when individuals cease to make exceptions of themselves and accept a position of equality under law. The laws of nature, no less than civil laws, are understood to bind all equally.

> For whatsoever men are to take knowledge of for law, not upon other men's words, but every one from his own reason, must be such as is agreeable to the reason of all men; which no law can be, but the law of nature. The laws of nature therefore need not any publishing, no proclamation; as being contained in this one sentence, approved by all the world. Do not that to another, which thou thinkest unreasonable to be done by another to thyself.[15]

HISTORY

In Books I and II of the *Leviathan*, Hobbes develops his scientific account of the state. In Books III and IV, he abandons the method of science for that of Biblical exposition in order to refute the claims of Catholics on the one hand and Puritans on the other that the state ought to be the servant of the church and accept the task of promoting the kingdom of God on earth. These last two books are usually regarded as no more than historical curiosities, but they have an enduring interest because in them Hobbes takes account of and repudiates the view that history is the working-out of a divine purpose and that men who understand that purpose ought to be heard in affairs of state. Hobbes argues that all such claims are fantastic, that they can be understood only in terms of abnormal psychology, and that they have to be dealt with decisively by rational men if sober politics is not to give way to bedlam.

In part, the struggle in Hobbes's day was the old one whether the church should dominate the state or vice versa, and the auxiliary one whether the church should be governed by local or foreign priests. The presence of radical protestant sects, however, gave the struggle a new, and potentially dangerous, direction. The Puritans who fled England to establish a theocracy in Massachusetts are a well-known example. Less well-known are the more radical Puritans (the Levellers, the Diggers, the Fifth Monarchy Men, and others) who remained in England, and who attained a degree of influence because they were part of Cromwell's army. Although many of these men were sound political thinkers who had sensible plans for extending the franchise and had no desire to overthrow or to weaken the political order, others were ready to abolish all government on the basis of their private reading of the Bible. The Fifth Monarchy Men, for example, maintained that the four monarchies prophesied in Daniel had run their course and that the millennial reign of Christ was at hand. They wanted to see Cromwell's Protectorate give place to a new system in which the saints would rule and the laws of Moses would replace the English constitution.

Hobbes perceives the problem that irrational political sects pose for those who think that politics has to be rational. His solution is the one already hinted at, that the head of the state must reserve to himself the right to limit the freedom of men to teach and to form associations. Specifically, in a Christian land, the sovereign must be the head of the church.

> For when Christian men, take not their Christian sovereign, for God's prophet, they must either take their own dreams, for the prophecy they mean to be governed by, and the tumour of their own hearts for the Spirit of God; or they must suffer themselves to be led by some strange prince; or by some of their fellow-subjects, that can bewitch them, by slander of the government, into rebellion, without other miracle to confirm their calling, than sometimes an extraordinary success and impunity; and by this means destroying all laws, both divine and human, reduce all order, government, and society, to the first chaos of violence and civil war.[16]

Hobbes presents an ingenious interpretation of Scripture, arguing that the kingdom of God referred to in the New Testament is not to begin until the end of the present world. The kingdom of God, he maintains, was the direct rule that God exercised over Israel from the time of Moses until the Israelites demanded a human monarch. Christ came to restore that divine rule, and it is that restoration for which Christians pray when they say, "Thy kingdom come." But the church is not that kingdom, nor is the Christian commonwealth (which, for Hobbes, is identical with the church). When Christ said, "My kingdom is not of this world," he could only have been referring to the time that remains after the last judgment; the remark has nothing to do with the history of men in states.

As we look back from the twentieth century, the religious fervor and the sectarian struggles in the time of Hobbes do not seem very important. We see instead the important economic changes, the rise of the middle-class, the passing of political power into the hands of merchants and bankers; we are aware of the New Learning and of the hopes of men like Bacon and Descartes that knowledge of nature is the key to health and happiness. Hobbes was living at the beginning of the Modern Era, when the bondage to religion was being thrown off and men were entering a new era of unlimited progress. Was he so disturbed by religious fanaticism as to be blind to these important changes? It is difficult to believe that he was. He was well acquainted with Francis Bacon, whom he had served as secretary; he had travelled in Europe and had talked to Galileo and to members of Descartes's circle; he was one of the men whom Descartes asked to criticise his *Meditations*. Hobbes was as conscious as any in his time of breaking with the past, and he had the same confidence in his science of politics as Galileo and others had in the physical sciences. Nevertheless, Hobbes was not carried away by the hope that man had entered on any great new age. What he knew of human nature argued against any substantial alteration in the human condition, at least as it affected morals and politics. This sober view was less exceptional in the seventeenth century than it was a century later. In Hobbes's day, enthusiasm was chiefly limited to religious circles. The Heavenly City of the Philosophers had not been announced.

VI

LOCKE

Property was one of the things that Hobbes made subordinate to the state. In the natural condition, he said, there is no property and no dominion. The practical consequence of this, in Hobbes's opinion, was that Charles I had a right to levy whatever taxes he might think necessary and that Parliament was wrong to reject his demands. History, however, was on the side of Parliament. When the Puritan revolution completed its triumph in 1688-1689, Parliament drew up a Declaration of Rights which stated, among other things, that the King could not impose taxes without the consent of Parliament. The next year saw the publication of Locke's *Two Treatises of Government*, which justified the revolution, basing its case chiefly on the claim that property rights are antecedent to the state and that the main purpose of the state is to render property secure.

John Locke had been secretary and adviser to the eminent Whig statesman, Lord Shaftesbury. Historians are now inclined to think that the second of the *Two Treatises*, the one that chiefly interests us, was actually written eight or ten years before the Revolution of 1688 in support of Lord Shaftesbury's ill-fated attempt to raise an armed revolt against Charles II. If this view is correct, it adds piquancy to the writing, which turns out to be, not a rationalization of a peaceful revolution but a call to armed rebellion. Shaftesbury was imprisoned, and Locke hid his manuscript. He published it the same year (1690) that he published his *Essay Concerning Human Under-standing*. But whereas the latter bore his name, the former was anon-ymous; and although Locke was generally believed to be its author, he denied it until his death. The reason for his reticence is hard to understand, inasmuch as Locke was on the best of terms with the new government. One must conclude that he found it embarrassing to be known both as a philosopher and a propagandist, and that he did not want to have to answer those who objected that his political ideas were not properly founded on the principles expounded in his philosophical work. A case in point is the law of nature, which is basic to the political writings, but cannot easily be reconciled with the teaching of the *Essays*.

ORDER

Insofar as the *Two Treatises of Government* was a tract for the times, it was mainly directed against the writings of Sir Robert Fil-mer, which supplied the clergy of the Church of England with argu-ments in defense of the absolutist claims of Charles II. The *First Treatise* is a refutation of Filmer's *Patriarchia*, in which it is argued that men are naturally born into the condition of subjects, that the king's authority is neither more nor less than the dominion that, from Adam on down, God has granted to fathers over their children. Locke denied these contentions. Suppose that it were possible for us to get Dr. Locke and Sir Robert together and put to them the question *Is the state natural or artificial?* Sir Robert would presum-ably say that the state is natural, and Dr. Locke, in order to give the theory of natural dominion the widest berth, would say that it is artificial. If, like good interviewers, we were to ask Dr. Locke wheth-er Mr. Hobbes had not shown that, granting the theory that the state is artificial, sovereigns must be absolute, we would be giving Locke the opening he wanted. He would explain to us that the family and other institutions (notably property) which occur in the state of nature are much more important than Hobbes had recognized; fur-thermore, that when men form the state, it is to protect these natu-ral institutions, and for this reason the state cannot be allowed un-limited authority over the lives of its subjects.

Locke's doctrine of the state of nature is not as clearly defined as Hobbes's doctrine is. Locke thinks of this state mainly in negative terms, as the condition of men who have not by their own consent become members of some political society. This is a broad category, which includes Adam as well as the newborn infant. It also includes the suppositious Age of Innocence of the ancient philosophers, which is not much different from the natural order of Augustine. "Men living together according to reason, without a common superior on earth with authority to judge between them, is properly the state of nature," Locke says; and this condition — he adds for the benefit of those who have read Hobbes — is not a state of war, but differs from it as much as "a state of peace, goodwill, mutual assistance, and preservation" differs from a state of "enmity, malice, violence, and mutual destruction."[1] But the state of nature also includes a condition scarcely distinguishable from that which Hobbes describes as a state of war — all that is needed is for some man to act contrary to reason, because in the state of nature every man is obligated to punish evildoers. In this way, war begins, with the right on the side of the innocent to destroy the evildoer, or, if he prefers, to enslave him. Nor is there any end to this condition in the state of nature, where every man is both judge and executioner. The slightest disagreement is enough to set men fighting, and the victory of the righteous is never secure. Therefore, men have the strongest reasons for leaving the state of nature and entering civil society.

Civil society, then, is artificial. Men enter it because the state of nature tends to deteriorate into a state of war. If all men were virtuous, there would be no problem. It is the presence of degenerate and vicious men that makes it necessary for the reasonable part of mankind to "separate from this great and natural community and by positive agreements combine into smaller and divided associations."[2] They do so by giving up certain of their natural rights to a civil society with the assurance that they can appeal to it for protection of the remainder of their natural rights. Locke is careful to specify what rights man gives up and what rights he retains. Man gives up entirely his natural right to judge and punish evildoers, and he engages to put his power at the disposal of the state as far as it is needed to insure that evil men are apprehended and punished. His other rights — to do whatever is necessary for the preservation and enrichment of his own life and the lives of others — he allows society to regulate, but he does not give up. In this way, the body politic is constituted. In the place of many men acting separately, henceforth one society acts as a whole.

When any number of men have so consented to make one community or government, they are thereby presently incorporated and make one body politic wherein the majority have a right to act and conclude the rest.[3]

Within the body politic, the will of the majority becomes the will of all members, somewhat after the analogy of a center of gravity in physical bodies:

> For that which acts any community being only the consent of the individuals of it, and it being necessary to that which is one body to move one way, it is necessary the body should move that way whither the greater force carries it, which is the consent of the majority.[4]

Locke specifies that no one is bound to obey the state except those who by their own consent, either implicit or explicit, have entered into the compact of incorporation. But those who have are "under an obligation to every one of that society to submit to this determination of the majority and to be concluded by it."[5]

As Locke interprets it, the contract merely binds men together into a civil state; it does not specify the machinery by means of which the state is to regulate its affairs. This choice of machinery is made by the majority, who may reserve to itself the powers of government, put them into the hands of a ministry, give them into the hands of one man, or work out some combination of these. Except in a pure democracy, supreme power (that of making laws) is placed as a "fiduciary trust" into the hands of designated members of the state to exercise in behalf of the whole. Even so, the people retain

> supreme power to remove or alter the legislative when they find the legislative act contrary to the trust reposed in them. For all power given with trust for the attaining an end being limited by that end, whenever that end is manifestly neglected or opposed, the trust must necessarily be forfeited and the power devolve into the hands of those that gave it, who may place it anew where they shall think best for their safety and security.[6]

The state, therefore, is much more like a business corporation than it is like a family. It was set up to accomplish a particular objective; and when it fails to serve this purpose, it must be reconstituted. Locke admits that men have a disposition for society and that they form families and other associations which may be called natural, but he does not pay any attention to these, even though (or possibly because) he was writing for Englishmen who have a long tradition of common law and hereditary institutions. For Locke, as for Hobbes, the state is an artificial body, fashioned by men to achieve specific ends. His disagreement with Hobbes is over the nature of those ends: Hobbes says that the end is peace; Locke says that it is property rights. This is an important distinction. If keeping the peace is the end of the state, revolution can never be tolerated; but if securing the right to property is the end of the state, revolution becomes a necessity whenever governments transgress that right.

FREEDOM

If Locke's book had been a philosophical essay instead of a political tract, he might have explained that he would use the words *liberty* and *freedom* interchangeably, and that he would use them sometimes in the negative sense to mean the absence of external restraint, and sometimes in the positive sense to mean the ability to achieve one's goals. He might have indicated further that in the former sense society restricts man's freedom, but that in the latter sense it enlarges it. Locke nowhere makes these distinctions for the reader, but he does employ the word in both these ways, and he does so with no more than the normal amount of confusion attached to the practice of using the same word to mean opposite things.

In some passages of the *Two Treatises*, the words *freedom* and *liberty* ring out with the same enthusiasm that they inspire in the revolutionary slogans of 1776 and 1789. Filmer's argument, says Locke, boils down to two propositions: "That all government is absolute monarchy," and "That no man is born free."[7] The subjection of children to their fathers (the right of fatherhood) was, for Filmer, the same principle that subjects citizens to magistrates. Locke finds this claim unbearable and lays it down as self-evident that all men are created free and equal:

> ... we must consider what state all men are naturally in, and that is, a state of perfect freedom to order their actions and dispose of their possessions and persons as they think fit, within the bounds of the law of nature, without asking leave, or depending upon the will of any other man.[8]

This view resembles that of Augustine, who holds that in the natural order no man has dominion over any other man but only over the lower creatures. Locke appeals to reason instead of Scripture to reach the same conclusion. Reason, which is the law of nature, teaches that all men are "equal and independent" because God has made all men and ordained them to do His business.

> . . . [therefore] there cannot be supposed any such subordination among us . . . as if we were made for another's uses as the inferior ranks of creatures are for ours.[9]

This is the freedom of self-determination or the freedom of anarchy, using that word in the neutral sense. But, as we saw, anarchy in the neutral sense gave way to anarchy in the negative sense of war and strife, so that men decided to limit their natural freedom and to exchange it for the freedom of citizens.

Locke's account of this new freedom is somewhat complicated. We quote the whole passage:

> The natural liberty of man is to be free from any superior power on earth, and not to be under the will or legislative authority of man, but to have only the law of nature for his rule. The liberty of man in society is to be under no other legislative power but that established by consent in the commonwealth, nor under the dominion of any will or restraint of any law but what the legislative shall enact according to the trust put in it. Freedom then is not what Sir Robert Filmer tells us "a liberty for every one to do what he lists, to live as he pleases, and not to be tied to any laws"; but freedom of men under government is to have a standing rule to live by, common to every one of that society and made by the legislative power erected in it, a liberty to follow my own will in all things where the rule prescribes not, and not to be subject to the inconstant, uncertain, unknown, arbitrary will of another man; as freedom of nature is to be under no other restraint but the law of nature.[10]

We note, first, here that the citizen is free because he has entered society by his own act of volition and consents to the laws under which he lives. Second, Filmer is wrong to say that freedom is living as one pleases and that men in states do not have freedom, because freedom consists in doing what law demands. In the state of nature, freedom consists in obeying natural law; and in the civil state, freedom consists in obeying laws of states consented to by the people.

In this sense, civil freedom is to be distinguished from subjection to the will of an absolute ruler, which is nothing but slavery. Third, there is a sense in which civil liberty is "liberty to follow my own will in all things where the rule prescribes not." That is to say, man remains under natural law where civil law is silent.

Locke is usually thought of as the great champion of the rights of the individual as opposed to the power of the state. There is but little doubt what answer he would give to the question as to whether or not the individual takes precedence over society. More than either Hobbes or Rousseau, Locke insists on taking the social contract literally. Since every individual is born a free agent, he can be considered a subject of the state only if he consents to it. A father cannot bind his children in this matter. Each man has to decide for himself what he intends. For most people, the consent is given tacitly: the person who chooses to enjoy any of the benefits of a state is bound to obey it. Tacit consent even binds foreigners as long as they reside in a country, although it does not make them full members.

> Nothing can make any man so but his actually entering into it by positive engagement and express promise and compact. This is that which I think concerning the beginning of political societies and that consent which makes any one a member of any commonwealth.[11]

Locke explains that this ordinarily takes place when a man becomes a property owner, inasmuch as states are mainly concerned with "the securing and regulating of property,"[12] and a man cannot hold property in a state without entering into legal contracts.

As a champion of individuality, Locke cannot help talking sometimes as if the state, however freely entered into, infringes on the liberty of the individual. In this vein, he says that man gives up the power of governing his own life "to be regulated by laws made by the society ... which laws of the society in many things confine the liberty he had by the law of nature."[13] But the citizen is bound not merely by laws already passed; he is also bound by future laws, that is to say, he is bound by the will of the majority. Here is the sovereignty which tyrants usurp. The majority of citizens must possess supreme power over the minority because the state has to act, and unanimity is impractical. The right of the majority is a sore point with individualists, however, who are likely to think anarchy is preferable.

Perhaps it is to sweeten a little the bitterness of giving up one's natural liberty that Locke sometimes talks of freedom as something that the state cherishes and seeks to promote. This is the Greek notion of freedom, revived and given currency in modern times by Rousseau, but hinted at in Locke also.

> ... for law, in its true notion, is not so much the limitation as the direction of a free and intelligent agent to his proper interest, and prescribes no further than is for the general good of those under that law.[14]

Locke uses very modest examples to support his view, such as the right of the state to fence off dangerous bogs and precipices. Subsequent champions of positive freedom (for example, T. H. Green, in the nineteenth century) argue that in passing laws to restrict child labor and the sale of liquor and to regulate wages and rents, the state is extending man's freedom. Locke is not generally noted for this kind of thinking, but he does say in the matter of bogs and precipices that law bestows liberty because "the end of law is not to abolish or restrain but to preserve and enlarge freedom."

JUSTICE

One way to avoid confusing the two meanings of the word *freedom* would be to use the word *justice* in place of *positive freedom*. Strangely, Locke does not have much to say about justice by that name. He speaks instead of reason and of the law of nature. There is, he says, no freedom except that which is guided by reason and bounded by the law of nature. This law is known to all mankind, and in the state of nature, it is man's sole rule. Since its precepts still bind men in the civil state, men enter the contract with the understanding that majorities do not have arbitrary power over minorities nor governments over citizens.

> Their power, in the utmost bounds of it, is limited to the public good of the society. It is a power that has no other end but preservation, and therefore can never have a right to destroy, enslave, or designedly to impoverish the subjects. The obligations of the law of nature cease not in society but only in many cases are drawn closer and have by human laws known penalties annexed to them to enforce their observation. Thus the law of nature stands as an eternal rule to all men, legislators as well as others.[15]

According to Locke, therefore, the reason for obeying the state can be stated either in terms of the logic of ends or of the logic of universals. States exist to promote the public good; they exist to enforce the laws of nature. Nor do these two reasons differ, if it be clearly understood what the public good is, namely, "the mutual preservation of their lives, liberties, and estates, which I call by the general name 'property'."[16]

Locke's theory of property is fundamental to his theory of the state. In fact, the main content of the law of nature consists of principles governing the use and acquisition of property. Every rational being knows these principles, and good men follow them. They may be summarized as follows: Everyone has a right to self-preservation, which implies a right to take the means of one's subsistence from the earth; reason teaches man to make the best use of the earth, to lay up stores and to tend the land; a man has exclusive right to the fruits of his labor, including title to the land that he improves; he also has a right to such imperishable wealth as he gets from exchanging the fruits of his labor and the produce of his land; when all the land is taken, those without land must live by selling their labor; criminal sorts, who will not obey the law of nature and choose instead to live by the rule of force, must be exterminated like wolves or other "dangerous and noxious creatures." All these principles hold true independently of the formation of governments. In the beginning all men were equal and the land was enjoyed in common, but God did not intend it to remain so. Both by reason and by revelation He showed man that he was "to subdue the earth, i.e., improve it for the benefit of life,"[17] which means that land cannot have common ownership. If man is to make the best use of the land and its creatures, these have to become private property. Locke is explicit on this topic.

> God gave the world to men in common; but since he gave it to them for their benefit and the greatest conveniences of life they were capable to draw from it, it cannot be supposed he meant it should always remain common and uncultivated. He gave it to the use of the industrious and rational — and labor was to be his title to it — not to the fancy or covetousness of the quarrelsome and contentious.[18]

Naturally, transgressors of the law of nature must be punished.

> ... the execution of the law of nature is, in that state put into every man's hands, whereby he has a right to punish the transgres-

sors of that law to such a degree as may hinder its violation.[19]

But protecting one's property became so difficult and exacting vengeance so uncertain that men covenanted to form states and resigned their executive functions to established governments. States properly constituted will not contravene the laws of nature but will make it possible for men to follow the laws more exactly than they were able to in the state of nature; states will help honest men resolve rationally their differences respecting property, wages, and the like; states will define various kinds of offense against life, liberty, and estates, and take over exclusively the responsibility for apprehending, trying, and punishing transgressors; states will assume responsibility for dealing with foreign powers; and states will distribute the costs of these advantages equitably among those who enjoy them.

> Political power, then, I take to be a right of making laws with penalties of death and, consequently, all less penalties for the regulating and preserving of property, and of employing the force of the community in the execution of such laws and in the defense of the commonwealth from foreign injury; and all this only for the public good.[20]

If the goal of the state is to make it possible for man to live by the law of nature, ought we to think of Locke as a goal-directed or as a rule-directed thinker? Probably the latter takes precedence. As to the question *Why should I obey the state?* Locke's answer would seem to be *Because it is right so to do.* Every man is bound to obey the law of nature, in whatever condition he finds himself. If he is outside society (as when a European merchant trades with an American Indian), he follows his own reason; if he is in society, he follows the legislative power; if it seems to him that the laws of the land contradict the laws of nature, he can emigrate; if he finds enough men agreeing with him, he can raise a revolution. But there is one thing that a man cannot do — either by legislation or by revolution — and that is to deprive another man of his property without his consent. Locke's theory of right is founded on his doctrine of creation and it is very similar to the Puritan teaching about work. God wants men to be happy, but they can be happy only if they observe the principles of work, thrift, and improving the earth. Persons who refuse to fit into the moral and economic system and who covet the goods of others are the enemies of the race.

Several questions now arise: What happens to natural equality?

Are not men born free and equal? How can this be reconciled with the inequalities of society? Locke's answer is that even in the state of nature, the working out of natural law produced inequality, partly owing to natural and moral differences between men, the results of which are compounded by their offspring, and partly owing to what we have learned to call the closing frontier — that is, the limits of real property — which forces younger sons and other dispossessed persons to live by labor and skill. Inequality did not originate with positive law but with natural law, and states are obliged to accept it.

Another question is: If the state is ruled by the majority of the people, what is to keep a propertyless majority from appropriating and dividing among themselves the property of the minority? We do not have a satisfactory answer to this question from Locke because reasonable men in his day (this excluded left-wing agitators) never thought of giving the vote to the masses. Were the majority to appropriate property, Locke's answer would presumably be that such a practice would be usurpation and nothing new, since the practice of governments robbing honest men is as old as cities.

> It is a mistake to think that the supreme legislative power of any commonwealth can do what it will and dispose of the estates of the subject arbitrarily, or take any part of them at pleasure.[21]

In the past, kings and oligarchs have chiefly offended in this matter, but the masses might do it too. Nevertheless, Locke is at fault for not being more explicit in his use of the term *the people*. He was not likely to be misunderstood in his own day; still, *people* like the *demos* of the Greeks and the *populus* of the Romans, is hard to limit. The history both of England and of the United States has seen this notion extended far beyond anything entertained in Locke's day. Not surprisingly, those who stand in the Lockean tradition often find themselves in opposite camps, according to whether they think property rights or the will of the majority is the more important.

HISTORY

It is interesting to reflect that, of all the philosophers dealt with in this book, Locke is the only one who was closely connected with men who held high government positions; he alone had experience in the day-to-day decisions of ruling an important state. At the same time, he is the first one we have discussed who actively espoused what in his own time had already come to be called a cause; and he went to great lengths to prove that his cause was based on the purpose of the Creator of the Universe. Locke's historical consciousness was not very well developed, and it is hardly correct to say that he was dedicated to the theory of progress, which had only begun to take shape in men's minds. But the main principle on which Locke based his political thinking is progressive in the modern technological sense of the word. Man, he held, has been placed on the earth for the purpose of utilizing its resources, and industrious and rational men ought to be given a free hand in carrying out what is really not man's business but God's. States are meant to expedite this work, not to hinder it. But this plan has enemies, people who will not follow reason; and, unfortunately, many of them worm their way into governments where they usurp the power given to them in order to rob honest men of their possessions. When this happens, people have the right and duty to revolt.

What are the rules for revolution? Precisely the same as those which govern man in the state of nature. Locke does not say much about tyranny and revolution until the latter part of the *Second Treatise*, but much of what he does say in the early part – about degenerate men who use force rather than reason and therefore have to be destroyed like noxious beasts – applies, and apparently was meant to apply, to tyrants. Political crimes are no different from other crimes and must be punished in the same way. If these notions seem advanced, we must not forget that the Puritans had already beheaded Charles I in 1649 and they had no inclination to repent it. The French in 1793 and the Russians in 1918 reasoned much as Locke did. The important thing is to have a theory in order to prove that the ruler is a criminal. Locke's theory rests on what he takes to be God's purpose in creating the world.

Locke's principles warranted killing only the enemies of property. Subsequent revolutionaries have not thought so much of property and have extended his principles to all whom they consider to be the enemies of the people. They hark back to the initial condition when men were free and equal, when all land was held in common, and when no man was beholden to any other for what he needed. Only when men began to stake out claims and to distinguish between mine and thine did trouble begin. Not the formation of states, but the institution of property was the origin of all man's misery, in the eyes of many, among them Rousseau, whose first published work was written directly under the influence of Locke.

If we ask Locke whether man can do without the state, he would merely point out the logic of his case: The state follows necessarily from property; property follows necessarily from the law of nature. But some who listened to Locke's account of men's original condition refused to listen when he tried to show the divine right of property. Why not abolish property and give man's social instincts a chance? No government would then be needed. Anarchists, such as Godwin and Kropotkin, for example, were to argue this way, charging with criminal usurpation those who claim part of the common holding for their own and making the state an accomplice in the crime. We can do no more than speculate how Locke would have answered the Anarchists' argument. He could not very well revert to the position of Hobbes, who traces the origin of property to the state, for this would require him to abandon the claim of the Parliamentary party that the state ought never encroach on the property of its citizens. Perhaps he would have been forced to give up his appeal to natural reason, take his stand on the traditional Puritan ground, and argue from texts in the Scriptures.

VII

ROUSSEAU

An apprentice engraver ran away from Geneva, found much un-
happiness, and astonished the world with his genius. Why did he run
away? Why could he not grow up to be an honest citizen and be
happy living and working with others? Jean-Jacques Rousseau was
the apprentice who years later asked the questions – and he never
ceased to blame himself for his youthful folly. It was small consolation to him that his name was known in all the salons of Europe, or
even that he was making a contribution to the literature and philosophy of the world. People who valued literature above the common
virtues were, in his opinion, to be pitied. For Rousseau, writing was
a poor substitute for living, although it was a means whereby he
might recover some small measure of the integrity that he had lost in
running away.

Rousseau's early writings, known as the *Discourses*, are an angry
protest against the false values of civilization. From them it would
be easy to conclude that the author was completely antisocial, but
this would be a mistake. Rousseau held that man needs society in
order to become fully human, and his later writings, notably *Emile*,
and *The Social Contract*, are an attempt to envisage a society in
which a man can grow up without becoming absurd.

ORDER

Rousseau makes a great deal of nature; that is, of whatever is uncorrupted by civilization and art. But nature, as dealt with in his writings, has two values, which must be kept distinct. The first value we may call aesthetic. Viewed in this perspective, nature has positive value. Man is happier with wild things than with highly cultivated things. Art is either good or bad, depending upon whether it is sensitive to what nature demands. The second perspective we may call moral. Viewed in this dimension, nature is neutral. Whatever takes place in nature does so by necessity. In the state of nature, man is simply an animal, governed by instinct. He is neither good nor bad, neither virtuous nor vicious. But man is more than an animal, at least potentially. When he forms societies, even the informal associations of family and tribe, he begins to develop capacities of the heart and mind that are latent in the state of nature. No longer governed by instinct but by reason and will, he becomes a moral being. In this state, he does not so much violate nature as go beyond it. Nature, whether in his own bodily constitution or in the world around him, becomes subordinate to moral purpose. Although Rousseau never loses his feeling for what is natural, uncultivated, and rustic, he is far from thinking that a return to nature is either possible or desirable for man once he has become a moral being.

If we ask Rousseau whether the state is natural or artificial, he is ready to answer that it is artificial. The only natural society, he says, is the family; and, strictly speaking, the natural family is dissolved as soon as the children are able to look after themselves. If families stay together after this time, they do not do so naturally but voluntarily or, as we say, by convention. That each man is naturally free and his own master follows from the law that an adult man, like any of the higher mammals, has to look out for himself; and this implies that each individual is judge of what means he must use to preserve himself. The reason families sometimes stay together is that the father governs his children for their advantage and does not make himself master over them. The paternal relation is not contrary to nature, but it does go beyond it. Slavery, on the other hand, is contrary to nature. It is wrong to think that some men are born to be slaves and others to be masters. Moreover, one is mistaken to argue that slavery is based on the right of the victor in war to do what he likes with the vanquished; for freedom is not something that man can barter away, even in order to save his life. In this way

Rousseau disposes of those philosophers who argue that political order is based either on the right of paternity or on the right of conquest. The state, he insists, is based not on nature but on convention. It is a work of art.

Rousseau approaches the political order much as did Cicero, who had to define a people before he could define the republic. There is, says Rousseau, an essential difference between a multitude of men and a society. A despot may subdue a great mass of men, but the mass never becomes a society under a despot because each man follows his own interest. In order to become a society, men must be united in a common interest; otherwise, there would be neither public good nor body politic. Even if a people give itself to a king, as some philosophers maintain to be the origin of government, a previous agreement must exist by means of which private individuals constitute themselves a people. This agreement, according to Rousseau, must be unanimous because "where, unless the election were unanimous, would be the obligation on the minority to submit to the choice of the majority?"[1] The true foundation of society is the agreement by the individual to surrender his private interest and embrace the interest of the group.

Nothing could be more artificial. Man's instincts are to look out for himself. Only when individuals find themselves unable to surmount the difficulties in the way of self-preservation will they consent to form a stable union with each other. Instincts provide no guidance when man finds it necessary to take this step; he must use invention. The difficult problem facing him is to get the advantage of concerted action without going against nature and becoming a slave to some other man's will. A risk is involved, but taking a genuine risk is not unnatural. What man must be able to do, says Rousseau, is to envisage a union in which he can give up his individual power and liberty and still have a reasonable hope of preserving his life and goods.

> The problem is to find a form of association which will defend and protect with the whole common force the person and goods of each associate, and in which each, while uniting himself with all, may still obey himself alone, and remain as free as before.[2]

Like Hobbes and Locke, Rousseau uses the fiction of an original covenant, explaining that it is merely a methodological device to uncover the presuppositions of every civil society. Men do all sorts of evil things in the name of politics, but insofar as what they do has anything political about it, there must be a residual understanding that the state is a means whereby each individual hopes to attain benefits which he cannot get by himself.

All of this has a familiar ring, but, as Rousseau explains it, the contract takes on a dimension that it did not have for its earlier advocates due to the two values he gives to nature. The political order is artificial, just as a house or any other human invention is artificial — Rousseau calls the state an artificial body, a public person, just as Hobbes had done. But the political order places man outside of nature in a second way. Men in states are moral beings. They do not function in the body politic the way that stones and planks function in houses; that is to say, they are not cunningly assembled by a craftsman who understands how to balance natural impulses against each other. Men in states have to be moral, discerning good and evil, recognizing obligation. Natural man, according to Rousseau, owes no obligation to his fellow; moral law is unknown to him, and at most he shows a kind of tenderness toward other creatures when they are in pain. Only when man enters upon a mutual undertaking does he recognize rights and duties, envisage himself and others as having worth, and grasp the notion of a good that outlasts the satisfactions of the moment.

When men first enter political life, they do not know what lies in store for them. They think that they are uniting only to protect their own persons and goods. But the terms of the union, not fully understood by them, demand that they rise above considerations of self-interest and devote themselves to a common good and obey a common rule.

> Each of us puts his person and all his power in common under the supreme direction of the general will, and, in our corporate capacity, we receive each member as an indivisible part of the whole.[3]

What emerges is "a moral and collective body" with its own unity, identity, life, and will. The contracting party is no longer an individual personality but a member of a corporate whole. He went into the state hoping to "obey himself alone, and remain as free as before." But he was only a savage then, with no understanding either of himself or of freedom. The marvel of man's existence is that he is able to rise above passion and follow reason, to rise above self-interest and seek the interest of a community. He does this when he forms a body politic and obeys the laws that he has a voice in making.

Is the state natural or artificial? After consideration, Rousseau might prefer to say that, strictly speaking, it is neither one: it is moral. Is the state more like a family or more like a business organization? It is more like the latter in that it is organized and that it exists to serve particular ends. If there are business organizations to which men devote their whole lives, so that they exist for the company rather than the company for them, the analogy is quite close. This kind of dedication, however, is possibly what some people think of as characteristic of family ties. The state is voluntary, but voluntary in a special sense.

FREEDOM

People who want to put other people into pigeonholes have difficulty deciding whether Rousseau ought to be classified as a collectivist or as an individualist. That ambiguity does not bother the philosopher, who is interested in developing general ideas and sees no need to give men labels. But our question whether the individual comes before the state is admittedly an attempt to get various philosophers to commit themselves on the matter of individualism versus collectivism, which is a lively issue in our time, whether or not it was in theirs. Hence the fact that some people insist that Rousseau is an individualist while others claim that he is a collectivist is a warning that we will not get a simple, straightforward answer. Hobbes and Locke see man as essentially the same creature, whether in the state or out of it, in each case prompted by the same motives, restrained by the same laws. Rousseau sees man as undergoing great changes when he enters the civil condition; thus, if by the individual we understand a moral being, the individual cannot be said to come before the state; on the other hand, because the state exists only to the extent that men are moral, neither can it be said that the state comes before the individual. Rousseau's statement on the transformation that man undergoes when he becomes civilized is an emphatic repudiation of the atomistic view of man characteristic of most political thinking of his time. "The passage from the state of nature to the civil state produces a very remarkable change in man," he says.[4] Morality takes the place of instinct, the voice of duty replaces appetite, and reason overrides inclination. Man loses some advantages, but the loss is minor.

> ... he gains in return others so great, his faculties are so stimulated and developed, his ideas so extended, his feelings so ennobled,

and his whole soul so uplifted, that, did not the abuses of this
new condition often degrade him below that which he left, he
would be bound to bless continually the happy moment which
took him from it for ever, and, instead of a stupid and unimagina-
tive animal, made him an intelligent being and a man.[5]

These changes which Rousseau describes as taking place when
man becomes civilized are hardly the kind of changes that we asso-
ciate with collectivization. In fact, the theory of collectivism is much
closer to the theory of atomic individualism than it is to Rousseau's
moralism, for the assumption of most collectivists is that man remains always a natural creature, dominated by instincts and impulses, and that what he thinks of as his will is only his strongest
desire. Rousseau's citizen is one who has become superior to this
kind of motivation. His state is the opposite of an agency for regi-
menting animals. The subjects who submit to the laws made the laws
themselves in their role as citizens. In order to think in terms of
laws, men must learn to grasp the universal in the particular. When
citizens in assembly decide that the good of the state requires everyone to pay a certain tax, they follow the necessities of reason and
not those of nature; and when, having returned to their homes, they
pay the assessment, it is with the same sense of their superiority to
nature. In this way, men attain a new kind of freedom. Each one
obeys himself alone, but he obeys only the rational part of himself.
All the philosophers so far discussed have had some difficulty in
pinning down the meaning of freedom or liberty. Rousseau does as
well as any. Immediately following the last passage quoted, he proposes to "draw up the whole account in terms easily commensura-
ble"; that is to say, in terms of *liberty*. In effect, there are three
kinds of liberty: natural liberty, civil liberty, and moral liberty.
When man enters the state, he gives up the first, and he gets the
other two in return; at least, he gets civil liberty, and he may get
moral liberty if he seeks it. The difference between natural liberty
and civil liberty is illustrated in connection with property. In the
state of nature man has possessions but no property, for he has to
rely on his individual strength to get and hold what he wants. In the
civil state, force gives place to right; a man receives from the state a
title to his possessions, and, if need be, the strength of the state will
defend his title for him. Property rights are only an example of the
many guarantees and securities that men obtain in states, and which,
from classical times, men have called liberties, even as they have used
the term free men to denote citizens.

But, according to Rousseau, there is a third freedom.

> We might, over and above all this, add, to what man acquires in
> the civil state, moral liberty, which alone makes him truly master
> of himself; for the mere impulse of appetite is slavery, while
> obedience to a law which we prescribe to ourselves is liberty.[6]

This third kind of freedom Rousseau excuses himself from discussing
at length because he has written about it elsewhere. But he must not
be taken to mean that moral freedom is not important to his theory
of the state. On the contrary, if the state is not to fall into those
abuses which are the worst kind of slavery, its members must be
mature, disciplined, moral persons. We are reminded of this when
Rousseau discusses the dissolution of states, which, he says, happens
when citizens become too lazy and greedy to take any interest in
governing their affairs and let them fall into the hands of magistrates, who should be merely deputies. Men must care about good
government in order to have it; they must put the concerns of the
state above their personal convenience and private business.

But though Rousseau is ever the moralist, he is not a perfectionist. In the first sentence of *The Social Contract* he says that he
intends to consider men "as they are" and laws "as they might be."
Moral liberty is, in Rousseau's opinion, a rare achievement. Precisely
because the state cannot depend on its members always to act moral-
ly, an element of coercion is necessary. The social compact, he says,
"tacitly includes the undertaking, which alone can give force to the
rest, that whoever refuses to obey the general will shall be compelled
to do so by the whole body."[7]

A man could vote for a tax and then refuse to pay it. Obviously,
such a man has not attained moral liberty, but the state cannot
compel him to be moral. He who evades taxes or breaks other laws is
compelled to obey because only in this way can civil liberty be
secured. This, says Rousseau, might be called forcing a man to be
free — a phrase which has caused some people unnecessary distress.
It means no more than that men being what they are, no state can
exist without police power. In some of his earlier writings, Rousseau
had taken the usual reformers' line of saying that rulers must be
forced to be just. In *The Social Contract*, where he considers the
people as ruling themselves, the same principle applies: If men have
not the disposition to keep the provisions of the contract, they must
be compelled to do so. Otherwise, "civil undertakings . . .would be
absurd, tyrannical, and liable to the most frightful abuses."

JUSTICE

The question *Why should I obey the state?* is similar to the question that a member of a hiking party might ask: Why should I join hands with the others in crossing this river? The usual answer of social-contract theorists to this question would be: I will be safer if I do. Rousseau's answer would be: We will all be safer if I do. To Rousseau's thinking, individual self-interest is not sufficient reason for obeying law. If the political undertaking is to succeed, men must be motivated by duty as well as by interest – or, more precisely, their notion of what is their interest must be corrected so that they can see that human goods, as distinct from animal satisfactions, go only with being a member of a group. Social obligation, as we may call it, is partly an expression of man's affective nature, such as we find in families. In its highest form, it is a disclosure of reason, such as we find in covenants and laws. Either way, membership in society takes man out of himself, makes him something more than he was in his natural condition, and binds him to his fellow by chains that sometimes chafe but from which he does not want to be released. Incidentally, this is the meaning of Rousseau's famous dictum: "Man is born free; and everywhere he is in chains."[8] People have taken this as a revolutionary slogan, but if they would read the rest of the paragraph, they would see that the chains are simply political bonds. Man gave up his natural freedom to assume the burdens of citizenship. "How did this change come about?" asks Rousseau; "I do not know. What can make it legitimate? That question I think I can answer." Obedience to the state is burdensome, from one point of view, but the burden is one that man cannot decently wish to be rid of.

In the example of hikers crossing a river, if one or more were to be swept away by the current, the whole party would feel their loss. That is the way Rousseau thinks that citizens should look upon their engagement to other members of the state. They do not cease to be private individuals with interests that others do not share; still, as members of the body politic, they have some interests in common; and, from this point of view, the good fortune or ill fortune of one concerns all the rest.

This conception of membership in a mutual corporation gives rise to the notion of justice, which Rousseau takes to be simply another expression for equal right. There is no such thing as natural justice, corresponding to natural liberty. In the state of nature every man is guided by his particular will. To say that a man (or a wolf) has a right to whatever he can get is merely to say that right and wrong have nothing to do with the case. Right and wrong come into the picture when the individual ceases to think of himself in isolation and begins to think of himself as one man among many. Instead of thinking of his individual good, he begins to think of a common good; or, what is the same thing for Rousseau, instead of following his particular will he begins to follow the general will of the group.

The term *general will* may strike us as strange, suggesting some doctrine of an Oversoul. Rousseau intends nothing like that. Philosophers (and politicians even louder and more often) talk of the common good or the common interest. Indeed, the notion is embodied in the terms republic and commonwealth. Rousseau wants to talk about the new frame of mind that is directed to the common good in order to contrast it with the frame of mind that is directed to one's private good; therefore he speaks of the general will as opposed to the particular will. The terms had already been used by Diderot in his article on Natural Right in the famous *Encyclopédie*, to which Rousseau was also a contributor. The general will, says Rousseau, is not an abstraction. It really exists wherever men form a genuine society, but it exists only in the minds of the individual members of the society where it has constantly to struggle against each man's particular will.

The general will gives rise to the notion of justice by teaching men to consider the whole body of men rather than simply to think of themselves as individuals. When a man sets aside his particular will to follow the general will, he does not sacrifice his good to the good of others, as it might appear to the individualist. The common good is his good too, and the general will is his own best will. The difference between the general will and the particular will is that according to the former, whatever a man wants for himself, he wants for all. Life, liberty, and security are good for him because they are good for all men. Insofar as he is sufficiently moral to follow the general will instead of his particular will, he wants these for himself because they are good for him as a man:

> The undertakings which bind us to the social body are obligatory only because they are mutual; and their nature is such that in fulfilling them we cannot work for others without working for ourselves. Why is it that the general will is always in the right, and that all continually will the happiness of each one, unless it is because there is not a man who does not think of "each" as meaning him, and consider himself in voting for all? This proves

that equality of rights and the idea of justice which such equality creates originates in the preference each man gives to himself, and accordingly in the very nature of man. It proves that the general will, to be really such, must be general in its object as well as its essence; that it must both come from all and apply to all; and that it loses its natural rectitude when it is directed to some particular and determinate object, because in such a case we are judging of something foreign to us, and have no true principle of equity to guide us.[9]

The statement "the general will is always in the right" refers to an earlier statement that the general will is both good and right. There Rousseau argued that the general will is good because it wills men's best interests, whether or not they know it. In the passage quoted above, Rousseau maintains that the general will is right because it is general; that is, because in it each man counts as much as any other: "...it must both come from all and apply to all; ...it loses its natural rectitude when it is directed to some particular and determinate object."

This last observation underlies Rousseau's contention that the general will can act only by legislating. Laws are generalizations; they apply to all men equally. States must sometimes act in ways that apply to men in particular: for example, in deciding on a man's guilt and in assigning a penalty. As Rousseau sees it, the general will, as expressed in the majority vote of the assembled citizens, can say that everyone must pay a certain tax and can stipulate grades of punishment to match different offenses against the law. In other words, the general will knows what it wants and what is the best way to get it — in general; but it has no special competence for resolving factual matters and should set up special administrative machinery for this purpose. This line of reasoning is behind Rousseau's insistence that the legislative power be retained by the people, who must assemble from time to time for the purpose of reviewing the common good and passing such laws as are needed. The general will resides in the sovereign people and cannot be delegated.

> I hold then that sovereignty, being nothing less than the exercise of the general will, can never be alienated, and that the sovereign, who is no less than a collective being, cannot be represented except by himself: the power indeed may be transmitted, but not the will.[10]

The power to execute the general will is what states find they must turn over to the government, which is an agent "to work under the direction of the general will" and always answerable to it.

Rousseau admits that states are fallible. The general will can never be wrong, but the people in assembly can be mistaken as to what the general will is. If the people are worthy of the name, genuinely interested in promoting the common welfare, the chances are good that the general will will show itself in the majority vote. What chiefly endangers states is the possibility that factions will develop which will want to use the power of the state for the advantage of some part of it. When this happens, members of the state have to obey a particular will and not the general will, which is, in essence, slavery and a return to the state of nature where might takes the place of right. In existing states, according to Rousseau, the people's indifference to the common good has made it possible for the governing bodies to usurp the role of sovereign and reduce the people to slaves.

For Rousseau, the logic of ends and the logic of universals meet in states, as he says at the beginning of his book.

> I shall endeavour always to unite what right sanctions with what is prescribed by interest, in order that justice and utility may in no case be divided.

The way in which he achieves this union (by construing justice as equality under law, and law as an expression of the general will) has important metaphysical implications, and Rousseau's account signals the dawn of a new era in political theory. Rousseau was a Deist and personally very devout, but whereas most Deists thought of God as the giver of moral law and the author of man's inalienable rights, Rousseau founded morality on human inclination and reason. No doubt he was preceded in this by Hobbes, but Hobbes never became popular in the way Rousseau did. Man, says Rousseau, is the author of justice; when man obeys right, he obeys no one but himself. It is to his advantage to construct a society in which in certain important respects everyone is the equal of everyone else. But more than that, it is a great personal satisfaction to be a member with others of such a society — to meet on the basis of common humanity, to call one another Citizen!

HISTORY

It may seem curious that a philosopher whose writings have inspired many revolutionary thinkers had no revolutionary fervor.

Rousseau's view of history was more Greek than it was Christian, or perhaps it was Augustinian, for he regarded Christianity and the idea of a purely spiritual fellowship as something irrelevant to politics, whatever merit it might have in itself. As we have intimated, Rousseau, though a moralist, was no perfectionist; and, in spite of his view that man is naturally disposed to virtue, he was no optimist and did not share the popular eighteenth-century belief in progress. Rousseau believed that a revolution was coming, that the oppressed classes would not endure much longer the abuses of the feudal, ecclesiastical, and monarchical order. But he saw no hope in this event because he believed that the masses were too demoralized to assume the obligations incumbent on citizens. According to Rousseau, there is a critical moment in the history of every nation when, under astute leadership, it can be forged into a people and a state. If the moment passes and they fail, they will never get a second chance. Even if they succeed (as did the early Romans), they cannot expect to remain static: a prosperous people quickly forgets its civic duties and allows itself to become enslaved. Thus Rousseau was far from sharing Robespierre's opinion that the mobs of Paris were the bearers of any general will. Unlike Locke, he did not intend what he said to be used as revolutionary propaganda.

Rousseau's thinking can be said to be tied to the idea of history in only one respect — what we might call his evolutionary view of man and of morality. Rodin's statue of "The Thinker," trying so desperately to pull his thoughts together and rise above his brutish condition, is Rousseau's early citizen. Reason and justice, human dignity and freedom, are all products of a great transformation within the human psyche; and, as Rousseau sees it, the social contract and the constitution of a body politic provide the conditions for the transformation. Indeed, Rousseau's view allows us to anticipate Hegel's contention that the state is the objectification of the will of man to be something other than a brute.

VIII

HEGEL

For as long as men have paid any attention to how the mind works, they have recognized in it a dual tendency: to distinguish between things that are ordinarily confused, and to unite things that are ordinarily distinguished. Practical thinkers find no problem here. But philosophers, who want to think things through, have to make up their minds whether their task is to make ever-finer distinctions or to look for ever-deeper unity. Those who decide upon the former tend to become skeptics (persons who claim knowledge is impossible) as, for example, when they press the distinction between subject and object, between knower and known. Those who choose the latter tend to become dogmatists (persons who insist that they have knowledge) when, like Hegel, they claim that subject and object, knower and known, are ultimately the same.

For Hegel, as for many before him, dialectic, or the art of making distinctions, is the special instrument of the philosopher. Hegel complains, however, that earlier dialecticians, including Plato, did not fully understand the nature of their instrument. They did indeed advance knowledge by distinguishing between form and matter, essence and existence, particular and universal; but they also arrested it because they failed to perceive that these pairs of contrary notions are mutually connected, for example, that the notion of form implies the notion of matter, and that form and matter between them

99

give rise to the further notion of substance. Fully understood, says
Hegel, dialectic discloses not merely the differences necessary for
understanding the detailed construction of the world but also shows
how these differences are related, thereby uncovering the intercon-
nection of all things. The goal of philosophy from this point of view,
is to trace the connection between the elements of human knowledge. Philosophy must be encyclopedic, in the sense of encompass-
ing the whole circuit of learning: the philosophical understanding of
any part of the world consists in seeing the relations between it and
the whole.

The philosophy of politics, then, turns out to be a subdivision of
the section of philosophy concerned with what Hegel calls objective
mind. Now, objective presupposes subjective, and objective mind,
which is the entire system of relations that we know as society, is
merely a working out in space and time of the thoughts and interests
of subjective mind, the previous section in the system. As Hegel
envisages it, the state is the highest actualization of objective mind,
but it is not by any means the culmination of the system. Subjective
mind and objective mind can no more stand by themselves than can
form and matter. In actuality, they combine to produce what Hegel
calls spirit (what we might call culture) — the realm of art, religion,
and science, including philosophy.

Hegel's political philosophy may be read in the relevant section of
his *Encyclopedia of the Philosophical Sciences*. In a somewhat ex-
panded form it is also published separately under the title *Philosophy of Right*. Both discussions treat the subject from a purely
theoretical point of view, omitting questions concerning the origins
of particular states and their special institutions and laws because
they are the concern, not of the philosopher, but of the historian.
But Hegel was also an historian; moreover, part of his claim for
dialectical philosophy was that the connection of ideas which discloses itself to the scientific mind also works itself out externally in
nature and in history. For this reason, Hegel's *Philosophy of History*
is also important for an understanding of his philosophy of the state.

ORDER

Hegel might have made a good press secretary for some president.
In fact, in his later years, from the philosophy chair at the University
of Berlin, he sometimes functioned as a spokesman for the Prussian

monarch. In any case, his philosophy is calculated to find something favorable to say about everything, and some word of caution as well. If we were to ask him a simple question, the answer would surely be either, Yes — but, or No — but. If we were to ask him a complex question, the answer would surely be, Both — and. In keeping with the principle of dialectic, any truth is at best a half-truth, except the all-embracing truth of the philosopher. Is the state natural or artificial? Is it more like the family or more like a business corporation? In some ways it is like the family; in some ways like a business — it has characteristics of each.

The state that Hegel undertakes to explain is the modern nation-state, not the Eastern-style despotism, nor the Greek or Roman city, nor the Western Empire. In his thinking, these were imperfect forms of society, only partially realizing the idea of a state. We shall see why this is so when we discuss the problem of history. Meanwhile, it is enough to keep in mind that the state we have to define is the modern power-state, solicitous for and sovereign over all its members.

There can be no state, in the proper sense, Hegel insists, except where men have already made great advances toward organizing every aspect of life. Families must be freed from feudal restraints; farming, industry, and commerce must be efficient and orderly; the public must be literate and the professional classes learned. In short, before one can have the modern state, urban society must overthrow feudal society and substitute rational laws for ancestral customs.

The state, Hegel argues, is the final step in the process of rationalizing society. The bourgeois family imposes rationality on marriage and property and child rearing, and in this way nurtures men to take their place in the wider society. But, in order to perform their functions in a rational order, men have to break away from the family and find places in business or in the professions. It is through learning to perform essential economic and social functions that a man takes on individual substance: he comes to know things that others do not know; he appreciates the importance of things that others do not value. Meanwhile, he understands that there are rational ways of resolving differences, and he is ready, when others are, to form associations and to submit to agreements and rules.

Hegel calls the social order brought into existence by the exigencies of a developing economy a *civil society* (although this translation is possibly too colorless because it does not emphasize the middle-class or bourgeois character of this society as well as does the

German expression, *die bürgerliche Gesellschafte*). Civil society could not exist without the modern family; no more could the modern family exist without civil society. The two are, in Hegel's way of speaking, moments in a single development, the goal of which is to integrate the rational individual in rational society.

But, Hegel observes, civil society taken as a whole is not rational, not even as rational as the family. The various private enterprises that make up civil society are extremely rational — a particular business makes efficient use of materials and labor and then markets the products to advantage — but none of the planning and ordering that characterizes private enterprise is found in civil society taken as a whole. Trades and professions should exist to satisfy human needs, but no provision is made in civil society to see to it that they do. On the contrary, in civil society, men use their skills in order to earn common exchange so that they can purchase the goods and services of other workers. This lack of planning leaves much to be desired. Not only do many needs go unmet, but the market is frequently glutted with an excess of goods for which no one has the money to pay. Hence, one commonly finds nations seeking foreign markets while their own subjects go uncared for. In a passage which will prepare us for reading Karl Marx, Hegel says:

> This inner dialectic of civil society thus drives it — or at any rate drives a special civil society — to push beyond its own limits and seek markets, and so its necessary means of subsistence, in other lands which are either deficient in the goods it has overproduced, or else generally backward in industry.[1]

Although civil society itself recognizes the need for laws and for some kind of civic administration, it conceives them as existing solely as a means for securing private wealth against encroachment and gives no thought to the problem of eliminating social evils or promoting the common good. That goal requires the sovereign authority of the state, which in one aspect (the Crown) must oppose civil society and speak with a single voice in the interests of the whole, while in another aspect (Parliament) it speaks for the multiplicity of interests striving for fulfillment.

Hegel rejects the social-contract theory of the state, and with it the notion that the state is an artificial body. Civil society may rightly be called artificial because it is devised for the realization of specific ends. But the state, even though it achieves the highest adjustment of means to ends found in any society, is properly

thought of as natural and organic. Its ends can never be fully speci-
fied because they embrace the best aspirations of all its members and
of all their particular associations. In that respect, the state is more
like a family than like a business organization: men are bound to it
as much by loyalty and love as by calculation and interest.

FREEDOM

Is the state prior to the individual or is the individual prior to the
state? In a philosophy that maintains the interrelatedness of all
things, it is antecedently unlikely that the individual is anything
abstracted from the family, the civil order, or the state — or that the
family or other society is anything apart from the individuals which
constitute it.

Hegel talks much about the abstract and the concrete, about the
universal and the particular; and the point of his dialectic is to
overcome these antitheses. The individual, considered in abstraction
from his place in society, simply as a man, a member of the class of
homo sapiens, is a nonentity. Equally barren is the general notion of
freedom, of doing what one wants, when it does not take account of
the wants of a particular individual in a particular environment.
Everything depends upon realizing the universal goals of human
striving in a concrete social and economic setting. As an example, if I
want the joys of companionship, the security and comfort of a
home, and the means to a good time, I have to be realistic and
accept the job at the telephone company, marry, and start a bank
account. To be anybody, in Hegel's terms, one must be somebody. A
young person, says Hegel, is likely to chafe at the idea of accepting a
particular place in society as "a restriction on his universal character
and as a necessity imposed on him purely *ab extra.*"[2] But this is
because his thinking is still abstract or, as we might say, because he
lacks experience. There is no real freedom except that which one
finds when one embraces the universally human in its concrete mani-
festations; that is to say, when one becomes a member of civil society and of the state, and undertakes

> through one's energy, industry, and skill, to maintain oneself in
> this position, and to fend for oneself only through this process of
> mediating oneself with the universal, while in this way gaining
> recognition both in one's own eyes and in the eyes of others.[3]

Hegel is sensitive to the various meanings of the word *freedom* and he finds a place to discuss each of them in his system. In general, freedom consists in acting according to one's will, but that entails knowing what one wants and knowing how to get it; hence, much of what men call freedom falls short of the actuality.

Objective freedom. The much-vaunted freedom of man in the state of nature is the freedom to pursue an undefined happiness. Man wants . . . he knows not what — and so, far from being free, he is unable to actualize any of his desires for want of fixed habits or firm resolution. Completely at the mercy of whim and circumstance, he is unable to determine his own life and is easily enslaved by anyone whose will is more determined than his own.

Subjective freedom. The freedom of indifference must, therefore, give way to definite will or purpose, which fixes on some goal and strives to reach it. This change ordinarily takes place within some kind of society. By learning skills and making themselves proficient, men achieve some of the things that they want. Moreover, in urban societies, where division of labor creates an abundance, men want and can have a great many things. It is foolish, according to Hegel, to talk about giving up freedom upon entering civil life because the more men's lives are organized — that is to say, brought under the guidance of reason — the freer they are, and this ordering takes place only in civil society. There are, however, limitations to man's freedom in civil society. For one thing, every man's freedom is limited to some extent by the freedom that other men claim. This is the consideration that compels civil societies to set up laws and establish administrations; it is on this account that freedom takes on a negative connotation, so that a man considers that he is free insofar as his neighbor does not prevent him from doing what he wants or insofar as the state does not prevent him from doing what he wants or make him do what he wants to avoid doing. But another, and ultimately more serious, defect in bourgeois freedom arises from the unreliability of the will when it is determined solely by subjective preference. Such a will, Hegel says, is arbitrary: it puts an end to the paralyzing indeterminacy of natural or objective will, but it does so by yielding to a particular impulse or fancy; hence, what it chooses today it may reject tomorrow. Many a youth has lived to repent, not his freedom, but his folly.

Actual freedom. For freedom to become actual, the will must be determined by the universal. Subjective preference must be purified; wholesome impulses must be distinguished from unwholesome by means of mature reflection and judgment. This goal cannot be achieved by one man or one generation. It involves recognizing the whole range of human impulses, learning their tendencies, estimating their consequences, and calculating their contribution to the sum of happiness.

> In this way reflection invests this material with abstract universality and in this external manner purifies it from its crudity and barbarity.[4]

Customs and institutions embody this universal estimate, particularly those of civil society, where

> individuals can attain their ends only in so far as they themselves determine their knowing, willing, and acting in a universal way and make themselves links in this chain of social connections.[5]

Thus, in a broad sense, all progress, all science, all technology, all education, everything that we call civilization enters into the fabric of actual freedom. There is no freedom apart from reason, but reason provides effective guidance to the will only when it takes concrete forms in morality and religion, in laws and institutions.

Hegel, therefore, is one of those philosophers who think rather slightingly of individual autonomy. To make good one's claim to be free, one must be a functioning member of a healthy society. Indeed, only thus can man attain individuality in any meaningful sense of the word. Part of the responsibility of the sovereign is so to organize society that there will be no pauper class and that every person will find a useful place within society.

Hegel's philosophy points in the direction of a welfare state. Does it also point toward totalitarianism? Hegel would have denied that it does. He did not envisage the state taking over the functions of the voluntary associations that make up civil society; on the contrary, as he envisages it, the legislative power of government should be vested in the Estates Assembly (part of Parliament), where the various interests of society are all represented. In line with his theory of individuality, Hegel maintains that a man's opinion is worth having only in the field of his special competency. Leaders from agriculture, manufacturing, finance, and all other segments of society must have a voice in government, but nothing is gained from allowing the people or their popularly elected representatives to decide issues of state. Italian Fascism was patterned on this aspect of Hegel's philosophy. However, it should be mentioned that Hegel had no intention of selling out the state to corporate interests. Indeed, the need for a state sovereign over civil society arose precisely out of the incapacity of corporate interests to take account of the common good. For this reason Hegel gives final authority to the Crown, which he envisages as truly sovereign because it owes nothing to any particular interest and therefore could represent the whole as no one else could.

JUSTICE

The reason for any man to obey the state is, according to Hegel, that only in this way can he attain freedom. Freedom is the key idea in Hegel's *Philosophy of Right*. As we have seen, the state is mind objectified: that is, it is the actualization in laws; in the moral consciousness; and in social, economic, and political institutions of the universal potentialities which, in their abstract and undeveloped form, are comprised in what Hegel calls subjective mind.

Subjectively considered, mind is striving for conscious self-realization. As Hegel describes it in the famous *Phenomenology of the Spirit*, the movement is dialectical. Beginning with the bare consciousness of an undifferentiated world, mind first disengages or alienates itself from things and from other persons and becomes conscious of itself; only then can it execute the return movement and recover its own being in its concreteness as a part of the world. The subjective process does not come to its final realization in the state, but in art, religion, and philosophy. These noble expressions of spirit cannot spring immediately from subjective want; they appear only when subjective mind has materialized itself in organized society.

Social philosophy, therefore, is the study of the material conditions of human freedom. These Hegel treats under three heads: abstract right or property; subjective right or morality; and social ethics.

Abstract right or property. According to Hegel, the first step toward the actualization of freedom takes place when a man appropriates to himself some part of his material environment.

A person must translate his freedom into an external sphere in order to exist as Idea. . . . A person has as his substantive end the right of putting his will into any and every thing and thereby making it his, because it has no such end in itself and derives its

destiny and soul from his will. This is the absolute right of appropriation which man has over all "things". .... I as free will am an
object to myself in what I possess and thereby also for the first
time am an actual will, and this is the aspect which constitutes
the category of property, the true and right factor in possession. [6]

When I have appropriated anything, Hegel continues, I have the right
to alienate it from myself by an act of will; that is, I can exchange or
sell it; hence, from the right of property there follows the legal
notion of contract. On the other hand, the possibility that my property may be taken from me contrary to my will is the origin of the
legal notion of wrong.

Subjective right or morality. Through property, man becomes
aware of himself, of his own purposes and intentions, and of those
of other persons. In this introspective moment man begins to attend
to the idea of happiness and to such related ideas as good, value, and
dignity. Also on this plane men form notions of duty and virtue;
they praise or blame other men's acts according to intention and feel
themselves constrained to obey the voice of conscience. Historically,
subjective morality is closely connected with the rise of civil society,
where everyone pursues his own happiness and considers himself the
judge of what is right. Typically, the bourgeois son affirms his independence of the family and his right to do as he pleases. But right, if
it is consistently and stubbornly private, is indistinguishable from
wrong; there is no crime that men have not justified on the ground
of good intentions and even on the grounds of conscience. To give
his private right any substance, the individual must advance to where
he recognizes a universal or objective right, which is what happens
when he learns to see that his private interest is best secured by the
laws and customs of his society.

Social ethics. Civil society is, however, more than an aggregation
of individual self-seekers. The intelligent pursuit of private ends
brings into existence a new form of life.

In the course of the actual attainment of selfish ends — an attainment conditioned in this way by universality — there is formed a
system of complete interdependence, wherein the livelihood, happiness, and legal status of one man is interwoven with the livelihood, happiness, and rights of all. [7]

Hegel calls this system the "external state, the state based on
need." It is an elaborate system of ends and means devised by the
pragmatic reason. But what intelligent self-seeking fails to apprehend

is that the system that it has created now takes precedence in the eyes of reason over the individual interests that it was devised to serve. Civilized man can realize his own interest only by serving organized society. In this respect civilized man is no different from his primitive forebear, who unconsciously placed the community above himself. The difference lies in the fact that whereas individual happiness played almost no part in determining the arrangements of the primitive group, it plays a major part in determining the arrangements of civil society. This relationship makes it more difficult, but no less necessary, for modern man to recognize his dependence upon society as a whole. Indeed, this difficulty makes it necessary for civil society to be governed by an external authority, the state, which looks after the interests of society as a whole. By recognizing the organic character of civil society, the state promotes the general health — regulating and stimulating the economy, promoting education and culture, and, most important, salvaging the derelict members of society who, because they have lost their property or lack education, have lost their rights and their freedom.

One point Hegel would undoubtedly make is that the framework in terms of which we have hitherto been discussing justice is too limited to take account of his philosophy. The two ways of justifying an act that we have recognized are reasoning from end to means and reasoning from universal to particular. As Hegel sees it, these are the two modes of subjective morality, for it is only the individual, conscious of directing his own actions, who thinks either in terms of the good or in terms of obligation. From the philosophical point of view, Hegel would say, the distinction between the logic of ends and the logic of universals collapses into the logic of the whole and its parts. The true universal is organized society, and the duty of the member is determined by the complex system of relations that define his individuality. Members of society are not equal in any but the most abstract and legal sense; the universal of class logic does not carry us beyond the consideration that all men ought to be free. Moreover, their duties are too involved to be reduced to the formula of ends and means, except in the abstract sense that the system exists so that men may be free. Actual members of any society have their duties defined for them by their place in the organized community. These duties are never precisely the same for any two men, nor for the same man on any two occasions, nor for corresponding individuals in any two societies. In short, what is right for an individual is always relative to the situation as a whole, or, as some philosophers say, to the total context.

Hegel's doctrine of the universal has interesting implications when we pass from the consideration of particular men and women to the consideration of particular states. Can we say that the various nations of the world are also parts of a larger system, and that there should be a supranational authority to harmonize and coordinate their affairs? Hegel balks at this proposal. States embody the organic principle, but each state must be sovereign and autonomous — no higher organization is possible, no international law, no world court of justice. The only court before which nations can be hailed, says Hegel, borrowing a phrase from the poet Schiller, is that of world history: "The history of the world is the world's court of judgment."[8]

HISTORY

The requirements of mind striving for self-realization can be traced in the lineaments of the state. For this reason, Hegel calls the state divine.

> . . . all the worth the human being possesses, all spiritual reality, he possesses only through the state. For his spiritual reality consists in this, that his own essence — reason — is objectively present to him, that it possesses objective immediate existence for him. Thus only is he fully conscious; thus only is he a partaker of morality, of a just and moral social and political life. For truth is the unity of the universal and subjective will; and the universal is to be found in the state, in its laws, its universal and rational arrangements. The state is the divine idea as it exists on earth.[9]

There is no such thing as right or truth outside of organized society, which has right and truth precisely in the degree to which it embodies the eternal principles of divine reason. But here we must take care. Eternal reason for Plato or for Locke is static, with principles that are the same for man in all times and places. For Hegel, reason is dynamic, disclosing itself first in one aspect and then in another. The same dialectical play which manifests itself in the structure of the modern state also reveals itself in the ebb and flow of universal history.

> Universal history . . . is the exhibition of spirit in the process of working out the knowledge of that which it is potentially.[10]

Hegel distinguishes three main moments in universal history, with characteristics that are easy for us to recognize by this time. The first moment was the Oriental theocratic state, which gave massive expression to the principle of universality: one people under one king, but only the king was free. The second moment was the Greek and Roman city-state, which gave expression for the first time to the principle of diversity, extending freedom to the many, but at the price of a disunity that quickly proved fatal. The third moment is the European nation-state, which combines diversity with unity. Christianity prepared the way for this new combination by disclosing the unity of the divine and human natures. In its religious form, however, the unity was, on the one hand, purely a subjective feeling, and, on the other, merely a transcendental idea. It remained for the modern state to embody feeling in institutions and so to bring heaven down to earth — "a reconciliation with the fulfilment of which the principle of the north, the principle of the Germanic peoples, has been entrusted."[11]

It should be apparent that universal history does not embrace the total history of mankind; like the City of God, it is selective and exclusive, the march of God through the world. One might say that Hegel anticipates Darwin's doctrine of the prodigality of nature: history turns up a superfluity of tribes and nations, only a few of which make any contribution to the evolution of spirit. According to Hegel, although every tribe and nation strives in some way to actualize the ideal, significant steps forward have been made by very few, notably by China, India, Israel, Greece, Rome, and Europe. These are the bearers of the torch of freedom, of the divine idea, and for this reason, they have a right that is not accorded to other peoples.

> The nation to which is ascribed a moment of the Idea in the form of a natural principle is entrusted with giving complete effect to it in the advance of the self-developing self-consciousness of the world mind. This nation is dominant in world history during this one epoch, and it is only once that it can make its hour strike. In contrast with this, its absolute right of being the vehicle of this present stage in the world mind's development, the minds of the other nations are without rights, and they, along with those whose hour has struck already, count no longer in world history.[12]

The absolute right which is accorded to an elect people overrides all those rights which are relative to the internal structure of society. Legal rights, moral obligations, social ethics "have their partial, though only partial justification" within a given state. But states are not bound by the ties that bind their subjects.

> World-history . . . is above the point of view from which these things matter. Each of its stages is the presence of a necessary moment in the Idea of the world mind, and that moment attains its absolute right in that stage. The nation whose life embodies this moment secures its good fortune and fame, and its deeds are brought to fruition.[13]

Can man do without the state? According to Hegel, no man can do without some state, but there are some states that humanity, the bearer of divine reason, can do without.

IX

MARX

The words *idealism* and *materialism* come into any discussion of Hegel and Marx. Hegel is an idealist because he maintained that no matter how hard one stamps his foot on the ground or pinches himself or how much pleasure he gets from the warmth of the sun or the smell of damp earth, he is merely entertaining himself with ideas. Marx, on the other hand, is a materialist because he held that it is necessary to start with man as a living organism — one which enters into numerous relations with its physical environment — and to explain ideas as the impressions that real things leave in his mind. In general, idealists reduce physical things to mental phenomena, while materialists reduce mental phenomena to physical things. The way philosophers use the words *idealism* and *materialism* must not be confused with the more common usage, according to which the idealist is one who believes that truth and right will conquer in spite of apparent defeat at the hands of those who pursue only material interest. In this popular sense of the word, Hegel was probably less "idealistic" than was Marx. Hegel seems to think that given freedom, most men are incapable of overcoming narrow selfishness, and that if they are fortunate enough to live under a strong and impartial state they should be thankful. The only genuine freedom he held forth was the Buddha-like freedom of the philosopher. Marx has to admit that men, as we know them, are narrowly selfish, but he believes that this selfishness is the result of bad institutions and, if the system were changed, all men would be as happy as Buddha — and a great deal happier than Hegel could imagine anyone being.

Marx early cast his fortunes with the socialist movement. As a student, he had to grapple with Hegel and to find some alternative to Hegelian philosophy if he was going to pursue the goal of helping mankind. In most respects, the system which he devised is directly antithetical to Hegel's. One thing he did learn from the dialectic, however, was always to look for a reversal: never judge the future by the present; if things are going badly that is good — the darker the night, the nearer the dawn. Marx did not live to see the first glimmer of a Communist victory. Some of his best writing is found in the accounts he gives of the failures of the Paris revolutions in 1848 and 1871; for Marx was able to pluck the rose from the cross and to draw from these failures assurance that future revolutions must succeed.

Marx was a great scholar, as well as a great propagandist, but his scholarship lay mostly in the field of economics. His philosophical ideas were worked out mainly in his youth before he found his stride. His papers from that time have been preserved and shed welcome light on the brief and infrequent philosophical passages in his later works. The celebrated *Manifesto of the Communist Party*, which he drew up with his colleague, Friedrich Engels, is the best single statement of his views on man, history, the state, and the world hereafter, but one needs to amplify what is said there by referring to other scattered passages, which are now available in several anthologies.[1]

ORDER

Is the state natural or artificial? According to Marx, every form of human association known to man is unnatural, even the family. If we want to recover what is natural to man, we have to go behind socialized man and reconstruct the human essence from man's biological makeup. We discover that man is part of nature, that he is motivated by drives and impulses, that he is naturally social, and that he has a peculiar need to "authenticate himself" by doing and making things. Human happiness, we might say, consists in cooperative enterprise. Men actualize themselves in work, by means of which they appropriate to themselves the natural environment; in the communion they have with one another in this work; and in the shared enjoyment of the fruits of their work.

Unfortunately, Marx continues, the communal life has not been realized. Men thought that they could satisfy their private needs independently of each other; they allowed the products of their labor to assume a significance independent of the creative process; work came to be looked upon as a means to an ulterior end; a system of exchange grew up; men began to work for wages; efficiency pushed them into specialized work; economic classes took the place of human society. Such is the story of our race. Marx admits that at some stages in history, society has been closer to the natural condition than at others. Contemplating the hard efficiency of modern competitive society in which money alone moves men to work together, Marx grows almost lyrical about the feudal estate and the guild system in which men had counted for something. His contention is that every known society has made the fatal distinction between the worker and the product, with the result that the evils of private appropriation and class distinction are everywhere present to some degree. Social organization, from tribe to empire, does nothing more than order men according to their work-function, and because the work-function has been fundamentally perverted, the social arrangements are perverted too. In the Hegelian language of the time, the worker was alienated from his product, from his work, and from his fellow worker; appropriation was alienated from work, men and women were alienated from each other; thought was alienated from action.

The state is one of the institutions that has grown up around the economic structure and, theoretically, it exists to take care of the interests of the group as a whole. In *The German Ideology*, Marx explains how social activity "crystallizes" into

> an objective power above us, growing out of our control, thwarting our expectations, bringing to naught our calculations, . . . And out of this very contradiction between the interest of the individual and that of the community the latter takes an independent form as the State, divorced from the real interests of individual and community, and at the same time as an illusory communal life, always based, however, on the real ties existing in every family and tribal conglomeration, . . . and especially . . . on the classes, already determined by the division of labor, which in every such mass of men separate out, and of which one dominates all the others.[2]

Marx almost admits here that given the selfishness of all human undertaking and the tendency for every enterprise to get out of control, the state is a good thing. But such would be too much to expect from fallen man. One of two things happens: either the government tends to take on a life of its own and pursue its own interests rather than those of the governed (Engels, in 1891, pointed to the American spoils system as an example) or it becomes merely the tool of whatever economic class happens to be in power (feudal aristocracy, bankers and industrialists, or petty bourgeoisie). In either case, the state is not what it pretends to be, and those theories are mistaken which suppose that men obey the state voluntarily in the belief their private interests are comprehended in the so-called common good.

In the *Manifesto*, Marx and Engels trace the rise of the modern European state to the development of the bourgeoisie. What we think of as political phenomena – such as centralization, uniform laws, national boundaries – are merely by-products of the growth of trade, the concentration of wealth in cities, and other economic changes. The modern representative state is, in effect, a joint-stock-holders' association serving the interests of the middle class, and its political parties represent the interests of different interests within the middle class. In such a state, the workingman has no voice; therefore the *Manifesto* urges him to form a party and to take advantage of the machinery of representative government to wrest power from the bourgeoisie. This new party must "win the battle of democracy" and "raise the proletariat to the position of ruling class."[3] The ultimate goal of Communism must be to abolish classes altogether, but to do so the working class will have to possess a coercive instrument. Afterwards, the state will count for nothing.

> When, in the course of development, class distinctions have disappeared and all production has been concentrated in the hands of a vast association of the whole nation, the public power will lose its political character. Political power, properly so called, is merely the organized power of one class for oppressing another. If the proletariat during its contest with the bourgeoisie is compelled, by the force of circumstances, to organize itself as a class, if, by means of a revolution, it makes itself the ruling class and, as such, sweeps away by force the old conditions of production, then it will, along with these conditions, have swept away the conditions for the existence of class antagonisms and of classes generally, and will thereby have abolished its own supremacy as a class.[4]

The *Manifesto* makes it clear that the state is artificial, but in view of the illusions connected with the state, it is too much to say that it is the kind of deliberate enterprise that philosophers have sometimes supposed it to be when they imagined men entering into contracts to achieve the common good. Men's loyalty to the state is largely hereditary, based on such real ties as kinship, language, and native soil; moreover, the state's authority is supported by the whole moral, legal, and religious superstructure that develops in men's minds and functions as a kind of second nature. But, although these ties give the state a unique hold on men's minds, they did not have anything to do with the formation of states in the first place, nor do they normally determine how their power is to be used. States have hitherto served as instruments of the upper class and of the middle class; and now, because the leaders of the working class know their true value, states will be used to promote the revolutionary aims of the working class, which are in reality, not the aims of any one class but of all humanity.

FREEDOM

Marx saw no essential conflict between individuality and conformity. In his opinion, it is meaningless to ask whether the individual or the group comes first. Society and the individual are abstractions. The individual, insofar as he has any character at all, derives it from membership in society. Man is transformed from a natural being into a human being precisely by acting within a group. "As society itself produces man as man, so it is produced by him." Even when a man works by himself, as a scientist or an author, his activity is social because it is human. "My own existence is a social activity." The community is what is real; my consciousness of being a man and having special characteristics is only "the theoretical form of that whose living form is the real community."[5] Pursuing this line of thought, Marx argues that in his natural (prehuman) condition man was not free because all his activity was the result of biological necessity. Activity becomes voluntary only when cooperation raises the individual above this level and gives him some choice in what he is to do. Marx complains that in society as we know it economic necessity has replaced this freedom, so that we lose the boon that social activity properly bestows.

Modern bourgeois notions of freedom are, in Marx's opinion,

mere caricatures of the reality. The only genuine freedoms Western man possesses are those that are rooted in the more primitive society of the Middle Ages when, in spite of class oppression, human relations were still possible. Commercial society has dissolved these relations.

> It has resolved personal worth into exchange value and, in place of the numberless indefeasible chartered freedoms, has set up that single, unconscionable freedom — free trade.[6]

As an economic historian, Marx understands the need for modern "forces of production" to throw off the fetters imposed by medieval and early modern states.

> This talk about free selling and buying, and all the other "brave words" of our bourgeoisie about freedom in general, have a meaning, if any, only in contrast with restricted selling and buying, with the fettered traders of the Middle Ages.[7]

But the change that gave businessmen the freedom they needed imposed a new kind of bondage on everyone else. Marx even denies that the businessman himself is free: the system of production and exchange is free, but the men who have conjured it up have no more power over it than the sorcerer has over the demonic powers raised up by his spells.

> In bourgeois society capital is independent and has individuality, while the living person is dependent and has no individuality.[8]

Factory owners are as much the victims of the wage system as are the workers, since they can survive only in a competitive labor market. The workers, for their part, become mere appendages to machines. When they go home, it is merely to recuperate for another day's work and to breed their replacements. With the improvement of machines, skill and strength diminish in value so that women and children replace men. The alleged freedom of a man to work where he likes and at his own terms and the corresponding freedom to hire whom one likes and at one's own terms are illusions, covering up the necessities implicit in the capitalist system. Marx consistently denies that by demanding an end to bourgeois freedom the Communists are taking away real individuality and real freedom.

Freedom and *justice* are not watchwords for Marx and Engels, partly because most people would understand the terms in the bourgeois sense, and partly because of the prominence given these words by rival socialist parties. The *Manifesto* is a radical document in the sense that it goes to the root of the struggle. Its authors clearly state that the interests of humanity are not served by the half-measures recommended by those who have no higher aspiration than to secure for working classes a greater share of middle-class benefits. Nothing will suffice short of abolishing the private aspects of modern economic society, but, say the authors of the *Manifesto*, this goal is not quite as novel as it seems. To a great degree, capitalism is already the social ownership of property: banks, industries, railroads, and the like are owned not by one man but by companies. Moreover, the kind of work necessitated by these great concerns is already social labor, with each job part of a larger cooperative undertaking. All that is necessary is to broaden the basis of ownership until it is coextensive with the labor force. Then men will not merely be working together, but they will be working for themselves and for each other. In this way they will recover the positive freedom and the kind of individuality that a man has when he is at one with himself and with his fellows.

> In place of the old bourgeois society, with its classes and class antagonisms, we shall have an association in which the free development of each is the condition for the free development of all. [9]

JUSTICE

For Marx, the idea of justice is purely a class notion. For the member of the proletariat who becomes conscious of his estrangement, "law, morality, religion are . . . so many bourgeois prejudices behind which lurk in ambush just as many bourgeois interests." [10] In Marx's vocabulary, these terms are ideological; that is, they are part of the conceptual system through which a particular social and economic order expresses itself in men's consciousness. In opposition to Hegel, Marx likes to insist that social change comes about not as a result of men doing what they think is right but rather as a result of the redistribution of economic forces. The religious, legal, and philosophical sanctions for change come afterwards, as men try to understand what has happened and to assure themselves that everything is as it should be.

> Does it require deep intuition to comprehend that man's ideas, views, and conceptions, in one word man's consciousness, change

with every change in the conditions of his material existence, in his social relations, and in his social life? What else does the history of ideas prove than that intellectual production changes its character in proportion as material production is changed? The ruling ideas of each age have ever been the ideas of its ruling class.[11]

It was impossible for the bourgeoisie (first Protestant, later Rationalist) to justify itself to the declining feudal (and Catholic) mind; nor was it necessary because its success was due to economic forces, not to moral or religious ideas. It is equally impossible (and unnecessary) for the proletariat to justify the revolution to the bourgeois mind.

... don't wrangle with us so long as you apply, to our intended abolition of bourgeois property, the standard of your bourgeois notions of freedom, culture, law, etc. Your very ideas are but the outgrowth of the conditions of your bourgeois production and bourgeois property, just as your jurisprudence is but the will of your class made into a law for all, a will whose essential character and direction are determined by the economic conditions of existence of your class.

The selfish misconception that induces you to transform into eternal laws of nature and of reason the social forms springing from your present mode of production and form of property ... you share with every ruling class that has preceded you. What you see clearly in the case of ancient property, what you admit in the case of feudal property you are, of course, forbidden to admit in the case of your own bourgeois form of property.[12]

The reasons for obeying the state are always ideological, except the reasons for obeying the Communist State when it comes to power. Communism is based, not on an ideology, but on the truth that exposes the self-alienating character of all ideologies. The true philosophy stands in the same relation to every previous philosophy as the proletariat stands to all previous classes because men who are the products of class divisions are unable to realize their universal human essence. In their condition of alienation, they turn to religion, philosophy, and politics in order to find wholeness. True philosophy unmasks these illusions and makes man "think and act and shape his reality like a man who has been disillusioned and has come to reason, so that he will revolve round himself and therefore round his true sun."[13] The proletariat is the class that is specially suited to be the bearer of the truth because it cannot afford illusions. An affinity thus exists between the proletariat and true philosophy because "as philosophy finds its material weapon in the proletariat, so the proletariat finds its spiritual weapon in philosophy."[14] Marx specifically connects philosophy to the liberation of German working classes.

> The head of this emancipation is philosophy, its heart is the proletariat. Philosophy cannot be made a reality without the abolition of the proletariat, the proletariat cannot be abolished without philosophy being made a reality.[15]

Marx always insists that the Communist state is transitional. Men will obey it because it is the instrument of revolution. Its citizens are no longer under bourgeois morality, but neither are they as yet under the fully human morality of the age to come. The enactments of the Communist state will be more "just" than those of the bourgeois state in that when the former passes a law, the law will be advantageous for the many rather than for the few. As long as the remnants of social classes remain, however, the Communist state will be subject to the limitations inherent in all political action. It will have to enforce conformity and compel obedience, always with a view to bringing about the end of strife and of the need for compulsion. During this transitional stage, the principle of the end justifying the means will be in force.

When the new age dawns, everything will be different. Then, for the first time in history, there will be appropriation without property. Stringent rules treating all men as equal will be abolished because men are not all alike and do not have equal needs or equal abilities. In the free society of the future, every man will engage in the work through which he finds the greatest opportunity for self-realization, and he will appropriate from the accumulated labor of society whatever he needs "to widen, to enrich, and to promote" his individual existence.[16] In that day, society will inscribe on its banners: "From each according to his ability, to each according to his needs!"[17]

HISTORY

The good news of Communism is that history as man has hitherto known it, will — or at least can — be brought to an end. The law of history is the domination of human life by the conditions of production. Work, which was meant to be a means of fulfilment, has become a curse. Alienation of the worker from his product, private appropriation, division of labor — these perversions of the natural relation give rise to class struggles and set in motion a characteristic development that, by an adaptation of Hegelian terminology, was called *dialectical materialism.*

The word *materialism* has two values in Marx's writings. Sometimes it is used to emphasize man's corporeal nature and the primacy of bodily needs. Quite apart from the dialectic of history, man is a material (in contrast to a spiritual) being. This use of the term appears in Marx's youthful writings. Later, the term takes on the sinister aspect mentioned earlier: history comes to be dominated by the modes of economic production and is intelligible only in terms of the struggle between oppressors and oppressed.

Marx does not deny that human impulses remain and express themselves in class society, but he claims that the conflict of interests between classes, not human impulses, directs the course of history; and, ultimately, an inner law of development makes inevitable the overthrow of the oppressors by the oppressed. This inner law he calls *dialectic*, but it bears only a superficial resemblance to the dialectic of Hegel. For Marx, the essential point is that the forces of production in a particular historical epoch create a characteristic set of institutions that he calls *the conditions* or *modes of production.* The forces of production have their basis in nature: they generate real change. The modes of production exist only as beliefs and habits in men's minds. Having no basis in nature, they do not keep pace with the forces of production, and gradually they come to negate the very forces that created them. Meanwhile, the forces of production generate more suitable modes that in time will overthrow the existing modes. In sweeping away the old modes, they are said to "negate the negation"; that is, they remove the hindrances to productive forces and provide new scope for them to develop. The new modes, in their turn, will become outdated and must be abandoned.

> We see then, the means of production and of exchange, on whose foundation the bourgeoisie built itself up, were generated in feudal society. At a certain stage in the development of these means of production and of exchange, the conditions under which feudal society produced and exchanged, the feudal organization of agriculture and manufacturing industry, in one word, the feudal relations of property, became no longer compatible with the already developed productive forces; they became so many fetters. They had to be burst asunder; they were burst asunder.[18]

Now the time has come for the bourgeoisie to be overthrown.

> For many a decade past, the history of industry and commerce is but the history of the revolt of modern productive forces against modern conditions of production, against the property relations that are the conditions for the existence of the bourgeoisie and of its rule.[19]

Marx cites as evidence for his claim the recurrent commercial crises, unemployment, pauperization of workers, bankruptcy of small business, and so on. Meanwhile, the proletariat is acquiring class consciousness, organizing, and becoming politically competent. Its demand for social ownership and social appropriation points to the only mode compatible with the forces of modern industrial production. The victory of the proletariat is as inevitable as was that of the bourgeoisie before it.

And then what? Will the forces of production continue to change, generating new conditions incompatible with socialism and demanding that it in turn be swept aside? If the proletariat should become exclusive when it comes to power, depriving any part of society of an equal opportunity to participate with every other, the dialectic would continue. But the proletariat is unlike any class before it. No other social system has so completely excluded the majority as modern society has the working class. For this reason, the proletariat is essentially a nonclass, a class of the classless, and thus it is the nearest that history has known to a universal human class. Its rise to power prepares the way for what has never existed before — a classless society. When, and if, that comes to pass — for Marx does not hold that it will happen of itself without men making any effort — history as we know it, determined by dialectical movement, will be at an end. It is difficult, if not impossible, for us to imagine a classless society. What we have to postulate is a completely new mentality, one that no longer has to negate the notions of ownership and the division of labor and class interest nor to overcome the opposition between individual and society, work and product, matter and mind because the unnatural conditions of work and appropriation have been eliminated, together with all bourgeois illusions. The classless society is the goal that Communists must keep in mind, the denouement for which the Communist state is only the preparation.

We have, then, Marx's answer to the question *Can man do without the state?* In his regenerate condition he can, but in his present condition he cannot. This qualification distinguishes Marx's revolutionary goals from those of other anarchist groups. The anarchists want to proceed immediately with the abolition of the state, convinced that once men were free from political coercion their beneficent impulses would come to the fore. To Marx and Engels the anarchists' view seems utopian. Instead of calling for the violent overthrow of the state, the Communists argue that "public power will lose its political character,"[20] that, having become superfluous, the state will wither away.

X

DEWEY

The words *intellect* and *intelligence* denote the same thing   both refer to thinking. They differ markedly, however, in their connotations — intellect is lofty and serene, dwelling in the realm of abstractions and forms; intelligence is swift and penetrating, at home in the world of people and things, alert to danger and opportunity. This distinction is basic to understanding the philosophy of John Dewey, who blames intellectualist habits of thought for the tragic lag between technology and culture.

The intellect is guided by what Dewey called *the logic of general notions*, and the intellectual thinker supposes that he has resolved a problem when he has found a universal term of which the instance in hand is an example. Instead of the logic of general notions, Dewey proposed to substitute *the logic of inquiry*, which is merely the way intelligence resolves practical problems. According to Dewey, the classical intellectual way of thinking is a vice, a perversion of intelligence, being a kind of escapism and a handy way for men of leisure and privilege to avoid the necessity of grappling with down-to-earth problems. The intellect is conservative; it holds on to old habits and beliefs and it perpetuates class distinctions. Intelligence, on the other hand, when allowed to function normally, is an instrument in man's struggle to satisfy his wants. With its help man extricates himself from present difficulties and anticipates new problems before they arise. The man guided by intelligence has no fondness for old ways of thinking when they do not prove useful, but he finds any way of thinking acceptable if it serves his purposes. He is progressive and even radical.

Dewey's criticism of intellectualism is partly directed against traditional philosophy; he wants philosophers to give up speculative problems and help men gain a comprehensive grasp of their moral and social problems. But in Dewey's opinion, those psychologists and sociologists who try to separate fact from value are also victims of intellectualism, the more so when they are unable to free themselves from the outdated practice of seeking universal causal principles to explain their facts. Intelligence, not intellect, is man's crowning glory. Civilization, particularly in its technological aspects, is the child of intelligence. Technical change constantly produces consequences, particularly social maladjustments, which were not included in technical planning – for example, medical advances have resulted in population problems – but it is childish to blame technology for this situation. What man must do is bring to the solution of social problems the same kind of trained intelligence as that which created them.

Dewey's philosophy is well summed up in a series of lectures given in Tokyo in 1919, published under the title *Reconstruction in Philosophy*. His position on political and social problems was subsequently amplified in *The Public and Its Problems* (1927), *Individualism Old and New* (1930), *Liberalism and Social Action* (1935), and *Freedom and Culture* (1939).

ORDER

One might infer from what has been said about Dewey's antipathy to intellectualist habits of thought that he has nothing to say relevant to our theoretical problems. We have followed traditional philosophy in supposing that theory and practice can be divided, that the philosopher can ask what political order is and leave it to the statesman to deal with the question how political order is best promoted. Actually, Dewey does not disappoint us. He treats of the traditional problems, but he tries to break through what he considers to be the tyranny of general notions and to restate the problems so that they can be dealt with by the logic of inquiry.

Dewey's attempt in the direction of what he calls the "discovery of the state" is a good example of his method. He complains that men have gotten nowhere in their attempts to define the state either because they have begun with the notion of discrete individuals and tried to explain how they unite to form societies or because they have begun with the notion of society and tried to explain how individuals come into existence. Freeing himself from this sterile controversy, Dewey directs attention to the consequences that attend different kinds of human activity. It appears that while some actions affect only the persons performing them, others affect a wider circle. In this way a divergence arises between what we call private and public interests. Men organize as a public, make rules, and appoint officials with a view to protecting themselves from the indirect consequences of the actions of individuals and groups. The public organized in this way is the state.

Dewey characteristically discovers half-truths in traditional ways of thinking. Those philosophers who started with the assumption that states are combinations of individual men, each seeking his own advantage, were not entirely mistaken: the locus of wants, choices, and purposes is always the single being. But something can also be said for the view that the state is a natural organism. Like everything else in nature — trees in a forest, insects and flowers, cells in animals — men act together. Association is one of the facts of life that does not have to be explained. What chiefly calls for recognition where man is concerned is the presence of intelligence; man observes the consequences of his conjoint actions, and he thereupon chooses some associations and rejects others. In this way man becomes something more than he was before, a moral being. The forms of association are innumerable. A particular individual may be a member of a scientific group, a religious group, and an athletic group, without in any way ceasing to be an individual. Just as each association is formed around a different interest, so it is with the association called the state.

> The characteristic of the public as a state springs from the fact that all modes of associated behavior may have extensive and enduring consequences which involve others beyond those directly engaged in them. When these consequences are in turn realized in thought and sentiment, recognition of them reacts to remake the conditions out of which they arose. Consequences have to be taken care of, looked out for. This supervision and regulation cannot be effected by the primary groupings themselves. For the essence of the consequences which call a public into being is the

fact that they expand beyond those directly engaged in producing
them. Consequently special agencies and measures must be
formed if they are to be attended to; or else some existing group
must take on new functions.[1]

Dewey tries to steer between what he calls the pluralistic and the
monopolistic conceptions of the state. Acknowledging that his view
has much in common with the former, in that it regards the state as
one of many forms of social groupings, he rejects the pluralistic
contention that the only legitimate function of the state is to settle
conflicts arising among member groups. On the contrary, Dewey
holds that the state may go as far as it needs to in regulating and
restricting other associations in order to protect the public interest.
One association has no more inherent sanctity than another —
churches, labor unions, business corporations are all to be judged in
the light of their consequences — and when any of these threatens
the public interest, the state has the right to take the necessary
action against it. On the other hand, Dewey does not want his view
to be confused with the theory that conceives of society as an organic whole, with the state as its highest expression, and other associations as subordinate members or departments of the state. Translated into the terms we have been using, Dewey seems to be saying
that the political order is indeed an artificial association into which
men enter for their mutual advantage, but that because men are
naturally social, other bonds besides the original intention help to
cement the political union.

In 1927, when he gave this account of the state, Dewey was
inclined to lament the fact that the American people was losing its
consciousness as a public — the problems before it were "so wide
and intricate" and required such specialized knowledge that men
busied themselves with private concerns and paid no attention to the
common interest. This situation led Dewey to call for better commu-
nication and freer discussion. He was willing to leave it to experts to
investigate possible courses of action, but he insisted that the public
must be involved in the discussion at the grass roots level and must
demand the right to make the decisions. With the stock-market crash
and the ensuing depression, Dewey took a more definite stand. His
main theme during the thirties was the discrepancy between the
theory of economic individualism and the facts of modern industrial
society. Businesses are not independent of each other; for better or
for worse, they interact with each other, and the consequences are

felt by everyone. Social interests demand that organized action be taken.

> We are in for some kind of socialism, call it by whatever name we please, and no matter what it will be called when it is realized. [2]

Dewey did not suppose that any simple solution to the problems of society existed. Politics had more and more become an irrelevant debate between spokesmen for opposing ideologies, while the nation drifted without any control. The creation of nonpolitical administrative agencies with power to regulate different sectors of society seemed to offer the most promise. The important thing was to grasp the problem in all its novelty and to bring every resource of human intelligence to bear upon its solution. This was demanding a great deal of the planners of the society of the future, but Dewey did not envisage leaving everything to the experts. As everyone who is at all familiar with Dewey's theories of education knows, his hope was to make the logic of inquiry (scientific method) second nature to all members of society. When this has come to pass, politics will disentangle itself from ideologies, and men will demand that their leaders present them with workable solutions to major problems.

FREEDOM

According to Dewey, one of the main obstacles in the way of an intelligent solution to the public's problems is an antiquated notion of freedom and individuality. The way in which these concepts dominate party politics and public discussion is a perfect example of the logic of general notions blocking the logic of inquiry. As the words *freedom* and *individuality* have come down to us in the tradition of Locke and Jefferson, they are defined dialectically; that is, they derive their meaning from their opposition to the state and to society as a whole. Historically, this derivation is understandable. When libertarian ideas were first fashioned, men were engaged in a lively struggle to disengage themselves from an authoritarian church, a tyrannical state, and an oppressive social system in order that they might organize themselves into new associations suited to take advantage of altered opportunities. The intensity and duration of their struggle made it seem that government and established order are incompatible with freedom and individual self-determination and thus encouraged the belief that every man is naturally endowed with all the resources necessary for his private well-being if others could be made to leave him alone. In our times, these notions have lost their relevance; and if our thought were determined by the dialectic of ideas, the truth for our time would be on the side of totalitarianism, which is correct in maintaining the need for social action.

According to Dewey, both the totalitarians and the libertarians are mistaken in following the dialectic of ideas rather than the method of inquiry. Because the logic of general notions sets the individual in opposition to society, persons interested in stressing the worth of the individual have been led to undervalue social action, and vice versa. Once we turn from general ideas to the experiential world, the antithesis between individual and society, as well as that between freedom and law, disappears. As Dewey understands the terms, both individuality and freedom signify the degree to which a person has been able to realize the potentialities with which he began life as an infant. Only in the trivial sense that the infant is completely unsocialized can it be said that the individual is prior to society. If the infant is to attain freedom and become an individual in the meaningful sense of these words, he must become an active participant in one or more human associations; and the freer and more democratic the associations in which he participates, the better his opportunity will be. For Dewey, democracy and community are practically synonymous terms.

> Wherever there is conjoint activity whose consequences are appreciated as good by all singular persons who take part in it, and where the realization of the good is such as to effect an energetic desire and effort to sustain it in being just because it is a good shared by all, there is in so far a community. The clear consciousness of a communal life, in all its implications, constitutes the idea of democracy.[3]

In Dewey's opinion, the changing times through which we are passing has created a vacuum in the lives of most Americans, even of those who stand in positions of leadership. The old individualism that built America has vanished, not merely because men today are caught up in a multitude of organizations, but also because there is "no harmonious and coherent reflection of the import of these connections into the imaginative and emotional outlook on life."[4] In other words, we cannot actualize our possibilities in the present organizational structure because we are not persuaded that we are coming to grips with reality. It is necessary, therefore, to think in terms of a new, constructive society wherein men are willing to face major problems and to attack them at fundamental levels. At present, we are caught in a vicious circle. Our outworn notions of individuality and freedom restrict us to the service-club approach to problems, which attacks merely symptoms rather than the ills themselves. For the time being, the service-club member is the best kind of individual that our society is able to produce because these groups are among our better associations. But when a genuine community emerges at the public level, when methods of inquiry have become second nature, when men learn to look out for their fundamental interests and marshal resources to solve problems in the order of importance, then a new, sensitive, alert, responsible individual will emerge, who is attuned to himself and to his environment. For Dewey, political freedom must go hand in hand with economic freedom and with freedom of thought, worship, and expression. But none of these freedoms is negative. The new liberalism of which Dewey is the prophet does not run away from positive action.

> Liberalism is committed to an end that is at once enduring and flexible: the liberation of individuals so that realization of their capacities may be the law of their life. It is committed to the use of freed intelligence as the method of directing change. In any case, civilization is faced with the problem of uniting the changes that are going on into a coherent pattern of social organization. The liberal spirit is marked by its own picture of the pattern that is required: a social organization that will make possible effective liberty and opportunity for personal growth in mind and spirit in all individuals. Its present need is recognition that established material security is a prerequisite of the ends which it cherishes, so that, the basis of life being secure, individuals may actively share in the wealth of cultural resources that now exist and may contribute, each in his own way, to their further enrichment. [5]

JUSTICE

The state, as Dewey defines it, is "the organization of the public effected through officials for the protection of the interests shared by its members."[6] As we have seen, a public comes into existence when men become aware of the undesirable consequences of the activities of individuals and of private associations, but it has to organize in order to curtail these consequences. "By means of officials and their special powers it becomes a state." [7]

From this account of the origin and nature of the state, we may gather Dewey's answer to the question *Why should I obey the state?* The intellectualist way of explaining states gives rise to the dialectic of command and obedience. This conclusion follows from viewing the state as the product of some will, either that of the ruler or that of the people. If we suppose the former, we are driven to conclude that the ground of obedience is superior force; if the latter, we are driven to the metaphysics of the general will or of an absolute reason.

> The alternative to one or other of these conclusions is to surrender the causal authorship theory and the adoption of that of widely distributed consequences, which, when they are perceived, create a common interest and the need of special agencies to care for it. [8]

Dewey goes on to explain his theory of law, which might be called a variety of legal positivism: "Rules of law are in fact the institution of conditions under which persons make their arrangements with one another." Using his own kind of dialectic, he shows that any meaningful cooperation between men rests upon certain assumptions.

> If individuals had no stated conditions under which they come to agreement with one another, any agreement would either terminate in a twilight zone of vagueness or would have to cover such an enormous amount of detail as to be unwieldy and unworkable.

This generalization is true even of criminal law, which, says Dewey, ought not to be construed as prohibitions but as conditional propositions stating the consequences of acting in particular ways.

> What happens is that certain conditions are set such that if a person conform to them, he can count on certain consequences, while if he fails to do so he cannot forecast consequences. . . . Conditions are stated in reference to consequences which may be incurred if they are infringed or transgressed. [9]

Those who object to the positivist theory of law usually do so on the ground that it fails to do justice to eternal reason and to the laws of nature. Dewey has no place in his philosophy for either of these concepts. The only natural law that pertains to man is the one that warrants every species to pursue its own best interest; and the only reason that man stands under is the one that enables him to profit from past experience. When free inquiry and criticism are at work, the laws of a society will be both natural and rational, in the same sense that the rules observed by tradesmen in their craft are natural and rational.

> Upon this theory, the law as "embodied reason" means a formulated generalization of means and procedures in behavior which are adapted to secure what is wanted.[10]

We could ask for no clearer example than that provided by Dewey himself of a philosopher who uses the logic of ends and means rather than the logic of particulars and universals to explain why man should obey the state. We have already come to know his distrust of the latter. In dealing with the objections that men have raised against positive law, he says, "Only if reason is looked upon as 'pure,' that is as a matter of formal logic, do the instances cited manifest limitation of reason."[11] In other words, when judged by the logic of inquiry, which measures truth by consequences, positive law is the very embodiment of good sense and sound judgment.

Dewey has but little to say about justice by that name. Perhaps he expresses the interest that most men have in justice in connection with what he has to say about equality, which is, in his judgment, inseparable from democratic community. Of the watchwords of the French Revolution (liberty, equality, fraternity), he says that under the individualistic theory of the state, the struggle for equality is reduced to an attempt to secure the same rights and privileges for all, an attempt that divides society and tends to lower the quality of men's achievement to one of mediocre conformity. When equality is considered in the context of communal experience, it becomes something else.

> Equality denotes the unhampered share which each individual member of the community has in the consequences of associated action. It is equitable because it is measured only by need and capacity to utilize, not by extraneous factors which deprive one in order that another may take and have. . . . Equality does not signify that kind of mathematical or physical equivalence in virtue of which any one element may be substituted for another. It denotes effective regard for whatever is distinctive and unique in each, irrespective of physical and psychological inequalities. It is

not a natural possession but is a fruit of the community when its action is directed by its character as a community.[12]

HISTORY

Dewey's attitude toward history resembles that of Henry Ford, who is reported to have said, "History is bunk." Presumably the great industrialist meant that only the future is worth thinking about, but he was intensely interested in that future, and if someone had suggested to him that in a broad sense history is the dynamism of human society, particularly the change brought about by man's organizing intelligence and the power man has to determine his own destiny, he might have withdrawn his remark. Much the same attitude applies to Dewey. Although he believes that lessons can be learned from the past, he insists that the future is rushing upon us and that it will be so much different from anything previous generations have known that their experiences can have little relevance for us. Dewey was just as much impressed as Ford was by the possibilities of technological progress. But Dewey's special concern was with social and moral progress, which he thought offered advantages as great as those of technology, and which he insisted must take place if technical progress is to be a blessing rather than a curse.

Dewey does not claim to possess any inside knowledge about the course of history. He rejects the doctrine of divine providence ordering the affairs of men toward a happy consummation, and he offers no theory of historical determinism to take its place. He refuses to accept the encouragement and consolation that comes to those who believe in the inevitability of progress and in the certainty of future bliss. According to Dewey, man's destiny must always remain precarious. If man refuses to modify his habits and beliefs in the face of the vast material transformations that are all but inevitable, chaos and destruction await him. There is no reason, however, for thinking that he will not make the necessary adjustments.

Dewey rejects the theory of class struggle and the call for a violent overthrow of the present order. The problem, as he sees it, is much too serious for such a simple solution. He agrees with Marxists and anarchists that human nature must undergo a radical renewal, but he denies that abolishing private property or abandoning political institutions will produce any such change. Since the task is twofold — to create a new man and a new society — progress must be gradual. If the new society is to conserve human values, it must be democratic, which is to say that individuals must participate in creating it; but at the same time, the only individuals competent to rebuild society are those whose intelligence has been freed from traditional patterns and has become accustomed to apply the methods of science.

Dewey does not minimize the size of the task.

> The prime condition of a democratically organized public is a kind of knowledge and insight which does not yet exist. In its absence, it would be the height of absurdity to try to tell what it would be like if it existed.[13]

If we are to know the direction of march, Dewey claims, we have to have a more comprehensive understanding of man's needs and capacities than the one that social scientists have so far given us. Among the unknowns is what life would be like in a nonpecuniary society in which everyone could have access to unlimited material means and in which inequality based on possessions would have disappeared.

> I am not anxious to depict the form which this emergent individualism will assume. Indeed, I do not see how it can be described until more progress has been made in its production. But such progress will not be initiated until we cease opposing the socially corporate to the individual, and until we develop a constructively imaginative observation of the role of science and technology in actual society.[14]

Dewey finds our best clue to the kind of man adapted to the future in the scientific community. Scientists have perfected the logic of inquiry, and they have constituted themselves as a community of mutually obligated and helpful members. The question remains whether mankind can learn from their example.

> Is it possible for the scientific attitude to become such a weighty and widespread constituent of culture that, through the medium of culture, it may shape human desires and purposes?[15]

The goal, according to Dewey, is a new culture in which the freed intelligence will refashion every aspect of life — economics, religion, education, art, and politics. Dewey did not, like many progressives, think that the state ought to work for its own dissolution. He wanted to see consent take the place of coercion, but he did not expect that the time would come when the public would not require an organization to look after its interests.

A major problem for populous modern states is that of keeping the state democratic. Modern communications provide the means of disseminating information and expressing viewpoints, but the danger is that public officials will use these media to deprive the people of effective control. To avoid this situation, says Dewey, local communities must be reinvigorated, and public issues must be reviewed in face-to-face discussions by citizens across the land. In this way government can be made an instrument of moral purpose; meanwhile, individuals can increase their personal stature by directing their own affairs.

Dewey did not want to be known either as an optimist or as a pessimist — another dialectical opposition of fixed ideas that arrests intellectual progress — but preferred to call himself a *meliorist* (from the Latin word meaning *better*). He allowed himself the hope that man is on the threshold of a better day, but he insisted that man will never see that day unless he makes a strenuous effort and unless he makes it before it is too late.

NOTES

Chapter I

1. William James, *Some Problems of Philosophy* (New York: Longmans, Green, 1911), pp. 15, 25.
2. Roderick Seidenberg, "Justice for All, Freedom for None," *Center Diary*: 17 (March-April 1967), Santa Barbara: Center for the Study of Democratic Institutions.

Chapter II

1. *Republic*, F. M. Cornford, tr. (New York: Oxford University Press, 1945), IX.590.

Chapter III

1. *Politics*, B. Jowett, tr., I.2.1252b28.
2. 1253a27.
3. 1253a19.
4. 1253a2.
5. 1253a37.
6. *Ethics*, H. Rackham, tr. (Loeb Classical Library: Harvard University Press), V.1134a26.
7. *Politics* III.16.1287a28.
8. II.5.1263b32.
9. III.9.1280a9.
10. III.13.1284b30.

Chapter IV

1. Werner Jaeger, *Paideia: the Ideals of Greek Culture*, 3 Vols., G. Highet, tr. (New York: Oxford University Press, 1945), Vol. i, p. 325.
2. *Romans* 13:1 (Revised Standard Version).
3. *1 Peter* 2:13 fol.

4. *The City of God*, V.12. M. Dods, tr.
5. V.19.
6. XIX.12.
7. *Ibid.*
8. *Ibid.*
9. *Ibid.*
10. IV.4.
11. *Republic*, Keynes, tr. (Loeb Classical Library: Harvard University Press) I.25.
12. *The City of God*, XIX.24.
13. V.24.

Chapter V

1. *Leviathan*, Author's Introduction.
2. Chapter 17.
3. Chapter 17.
4. Chapter 13.
5. Chapter 17.
6. Chapter 20.
7. Chapter 21.
8. Chapter 6.
9. Chapter 14.
10. Chapter 14.
11. Chapter 14.
12. Chapter 26.
13. Chapter 15.
14. Chapter 15.
15. Chapter 26.
16. Chapter 36.

Chapter VI

1. John Locke, *Two Treatises of Government*, Peter Laslett, ed. (Cambridge University Press, 1960), *Second Treatise*, Section 19.
2. Section 128.
3. Section 95.
4. Section 96.
5. Section 97.
6. Section 149.
7. *First Treatise*, Section 2.
8. *Second Treatise*, Section 4.
9. Section 6.
10. Section 22.

11. Section 122.
12. Section 120.
13. Section 129.
14. Section 57.
15. Section 135.
16. Section 123.
17. Section 32.
18. Section 34.
19. Section 7.
20. Section 3.
21. Section 138.

Chapter VII

1. *The Social Contract and Other Discourses*, G. D. H. Cole, tr. (Everyman's Library: Dutton, 1913), I.5.
2. I.6.
3. I.6.
4. I.8.
5. I.8.
6. I.8.
7. I.7.
8. I.1.
9. II.4.
10. II.1.

Chapter VIII

1. *Philosophy of Right*, T. M. Knox, tr. (New York: Oxford University Press, 1942), paragraph 246.
2. Paragraph 207.
3. Paragraph 207.
4. Paragraph 20.
5. Paragraph 187.
6. Paragraphs 41, 44, 45.
7. Paragraph 183.
8. Paragraph 340.
9. *Philosophy of History*, J. Sibree, tr., Introduction, Part III, Section 2.
10. *Ibid.*, Section 1.
11. *Philosophy of Right*, paragraph 358.
12. Paragraph 347.
13. Paragraph 345.

Chapter IX

1. References here will be made to two of these. *Marx and Engels, Basic Writings on Politics and Philosophy*, L. S. Feuer, ed. (Anchor Books, 1959). Erich Fromm, *Marx's Concept of Man*, with a translation from Marx's Economic and Philosophical Manuscripts by T. B. Bottomore (Frederick Ungar, 1966).
2. *German Ideology*. Feuer, p. 254 f.; Fromm, p. 206 f.
3. *Manifesto* Feuer, p. 28.
4. *Ibid.*, p. 29.
5. *Economic and Philosophical Manuscripts*, Fromm, p. 129 f.
6. *Manifesto*, Feuer, p. 9.
7. *Ibid.*, p. 22 f.
8. *Ibid.*, p. 22.
9. *Ibid.*, p. 29.
10. *Ibid.*, p. 18.
11. *Ibid.*, p. 26.
12. *Ibid.* p. 24.
13. *Toward the Critique of Hegel's Philosophy of Right*, Feuer, p. 263.
14. *Ibid.*, p. 265.
15. *Ibid.*, p. 266.
16. *Manifesto*, Feuer, p. 22.
17. *Critique of the Gotha Program*, Feuer, p. 119.
18. *Manifesto*, Feuer, p. 12.
19. *Ibid.*, p. 13.
20. *Ibid.*, p. 29.

Chapter X

1. *The Public and Its Problems* (New York: Holt, 1927), p. 27.
2. *Individualism Old and New* (New York: Putnam's, 1930), p. 119.
3. *The Public and Its Problems*, p. 149.
4. *Individualism Old and New*, p. 82.
5. *Liberalism and Social Action* (New York: Putnam's, 1935), p. 56 f.
6. *The Public and Its Problems*, p. 33.
7. *Ibid.*, p. 67.
8. *Ibid.*, p. 54.
9. *Ibid.*, p. 55.
10. *Ibid.*, p. 57.
11. *Ibid.*, p. 57.
12. *Ibid.*, p. 150 f.
13. *Ibid.*, p. 166.
14. *Individualism Old and New*, p. 99.
15. *Freedom and Culture* (New York: Putnam's, 1939), p. 141 f.

DISCUSSION
QUESTIONS

1. Distinguish between the problems which interest political philosophers and those which interest political scientists.

2. To what extent are your politically minded friends concerned with philosophical issues?

3. The terms *liberal* and *conservative* are used but sparingly in this book. Do these terms designate different philosophical positions? If not, what do they designate?

4. Do you prefer to speak of civil rights or of civil liberties? Explain your preference.

5. Define *utopian*. To which philosophers, if any, would you apply the term?

6. Is enlightened self-interest a sufficient basis for political association? Why or why not?

7. Is political morality essentially different from private morality? Why? Which philosophers could you call upon to support your answer?

8. Compare the doctrine of natural rights in Aristotle and in Locke.

9. Some scholars would hold that Plato, Aristotle, and Augustine form a single group; Hobbes, Locke, and Rousseau a second group; and Hegel, Marx, and Dewey a third group. Would you agree? If not, what groupings would you suggest? And on what basis?

ADDITIONAL
READINGS

Acton, H. B. *The Future of an Illusion*, 1955.

Adler, Mortimer, editor. *The Great Ideas, A Syntopicon of Great Books of the Western World*, 1952. (See articles on Government, History, Law, Liberty, Progress, and State.)

Camus, Albert. *The Rebel*, 1959.

Carritt, E. F. *Morals and Politics*, 1935.

Cassirer, Ernst. *The Myth of the State*, 1946.

———. *The Problem of Jean Jacques Rousseau*, 1954.

Cornford, F. M., translator. *The Republic of Plato*, 1941.

Deane, Herbert A. *The Political and Social Ideas of St. Augustine*, 1963.

Edwards, Paul, editor. *The Encyclopedia of Philosophy*, 1967. (See article on Political Philosophy; also articles on individual philosophers with current bibliographies following each article.)

Friedrich, Carl J. *An Introduction to Political Theory*, 1967.

Lowith, Karl. *From Hegel to Nietzsche*, 1964.

Mabbott, J. D. *The State and the Citizen*, 1948.

MacPherson, C. B. *The Political Theory of Possessive Individualism*, 1962.

Marcuse, Herbert. *Reason and Revolution*, 1954.

Maritain, Jacques. *Man and the State*, 1951.

Popper, Karl R. *The Open Society and Its Enemies*, 1950.

Quinton, Anthony, editor. *Political Philosophy*, 1967. (See especially the editor's introduction.)

Tussman, Joseph. *Obligation and the Body Politic*, 1960.

Voegelin, Eric. *The New Science of Politics*, 1952.

Weldon, T. D. *The Vocabulary of Politics*, 1953.

INDEX